PHILIP GOULD
An Unfinished Life

'In his politics, this warm, exuberant, confrontational man would suddenly ask the spiky question, the really awkward one. His last battle was extraordinarily brave; but it was when he opened his arms to death, and looked it in the face, that he shook everyone he knew – and a host of friends he never met.' **Andrew Marr**

'Philip was simply the best political analyst of his day. His genius was to be able to spot what others couldn't in the mass of data, make sense of it all and then define the way forward. He wasn't just my pollster. He was my pathfinder.' **Tony Blair**

'The greatest professional compliment I can pay Philip is that he was a disaster for the Conservative Party – helping to mastermind campaigns that inflicted three electoral defeats on us. The greatest personal compliment is that he set aside partisan conflict whenever we spoke to each other. It was clear from our conversations that what motivated him was a genuine, passionate desire to improve his world. My last memory of Philip is also my fondest. He and Gail gave me a lift back from a conference which we had all been attending because I didn't have a car, and sitting in the back seat I received a brilliant analysis of all the things the then Conservative Opposition were doing right, and doing wrong. It would be hard to find a better analysis today.' **George Osborne**

'Philip was a truly exceptional man with extraordinary talents. He was a pathbreaking political strategist as well as a warm, funny, engaging, deeply emotional and loving human being. Nowhere was he more extraordinary than in the final years of his life: battling his cancer like a political campaign that could be mastered and won. Then accepting death with courage and bravery. His contribution to Labour politics was enormous. His work and commitment helped change the lives of millions of his fellow citizens for the better. By helping Labour to win three elections, he helped rebuild our schools, save our NHS and repair the fabric of Britain. Many who benefit will never know his name but will have better lives in part because of his work. In an age when people are cynical about politics, he was someone who was in it for the best of reasons: because of his deep rooted concern for the people of Britain and his wish to make Labour their voice. His memory will live on in his wonderful family and all those who had the privilege to call him their friend.' **Ed Miliband**

PHILIP GOULD
An Unfinished Life

Edited by Dennis Kavanagh

palgrave
macmillan

First published 2012 by
PALGRAVE MACMILLAN

Palgrave Macmillan in the UK is an imprint of Macmillan Publishers Limited,
registered in England, company number 785998, of Houndmills, Basingstoke,
Hampshire RG21 6XS.

Palgrave Macmillan in the US is a division of St Martin's Press LLC,
175 Fifth Avenue, New York, NY 10010.

Palgrave Macmillan is the global academic imprint of the above companies
and has companies and representatives throughout the world.

Palgrave® and Macmillan® are registered trademarks in the United States,
the United Kingdom, Europe and other countries

ISBN: 978-1-137-28112-8   hardback

This book is printed on paper suitable for recycling and made from fully
managed and sustained forest sources. Logging, pulping and manufacturing
processes are expected to conform to the environmental regulations of the
country of origin.

A catalogue record for this book is available from the British Library.

A catalog record for this book is available from the Library of Congress.

10 9 8 7 6 5 4 3 2 1
21 20 19 18 17 16 15 14 13 12

Printed and bound in Great Britain by
CPI Antony Rowe, Chippenham and Eastbourne

Contents

Preface

Dennis Kavanagh

My last conversation with Philip Gould took place a few weeks before he died. At home in his favourite room, overlooking Regent's Park, he did most of the talking. We covered politics, his family, what to do about his papers and diaries, and his preparations for his death. Near the end I asked how he would feel if somebody organised a book about his life and work. He responded with enthusiasm, and Philip, when enthusiastic, was a sight to behold. He started to pace the room and throw out names and ideas. I said that if I was involved, such a book should go beyond the Blair–Brown rivalry and the problems of the Labour Party. We agreed on this and planned to meet again. As I left he gave me a signed copy of his revised *The Unfinished Revolution*. He scribbled an inscription, the last sentences of which read 'It has been a joint journey, not yet finished. I am sure we will have several opportunities to meet in the future.' He thought he had more time. He did not.

Without Philip, but with the support of his family, I proceeded. Despite my initial doubts, everybody I approached accepted immediately, two saying they felt 'honoured'. And then I had doubts that everybody would actually deliver. They did, making my task an easy one. That the contributors with their many commitments cooperated so readily was a mark of their admiration and affection for Philip. He would have been delighted and even humbled with this book.

Amber Stone-Galilee has been a supportive and encouraging editor. My thanks go to her and the staff at Palgrave Macmillan.

All proceeds from the Sale of this book will go to the National Oesophago-Gastric Cancer Fund, and The Royal Marsden Cancer Charity.

Philip Gould's papers have been deposited at Churchill College, Cambridge University.

Notes on Contributors

Alastair Campbell became Tony Blair's press secretary in 1994, was his spokesman and strategist full time until 2003, and returned as communications director for the 2005 election. He was a key player in Labour's three election victories and the major issues of the Blair government. He now writes, speaks, consults and works for charities dedicated to mental illness and leukaemia. He has written eight books since leaving Downing Street: five volumes of diaries, two novels and a personal memoir on depression.

Andrew Cooper is Director of Strategy to Prime Minister David Cameron. He is co-founder of the research consultancy Populus and previously worked for the Conservative Party from 1995 to 1999 and for the Social Market Foundation.

Danny Finkelstein is Executive Editor of *The Times* and a weekly columnist for the paper. In 1995 he went to work for John Major as the director of the Conservative Research Department and stayed after William Hague became leader, becoming his chief policy adviser.

Georgia Gould is Philip Gould's eldest daughter. An Oxford graduate in history and politics, a Labour councillor and former full-time organiser, she has also worked for the Tony Blair Faith Foundation and is currently working on a number of projects around educational disadvantage and youth unemployment in Camden.

Stanley Greenberg is a leading US Democrat pollster and strategist and head of Greenberg, Quinlan Rosner. He was pollster for Bill Clinton in the 1992 Presidential campaign and for the Labour Party in 1997, 2001 and 2005 and with James Morris, continues in that role for Labour under Ed Miliband. He has just published, with James Carville, *It's the Middle Class Stupid!*

James Harding has been the Editor of *The Times* since 2007, having joined the paper in 2006. He previously worked for the *Financial Times* in London, Shanghai and Washington.

Patricia Hewitt was Labour MP for Leicester West from 1997 to 2010. She served in Tony Blair's Cabinet as Secretary of State for Trade and Industry, Cabinet Minister for Women and Secretary of State for Health. She is now senior independent director of BT, chair of the UK India Business Council and works with a Delhi-based charity, Katha.

Peter Hyman is Headteacher of School 21, a new 4–18 school in Stratford, East London. Between 1994 and 2003 he was political strategist and speechwriter to Tony Blair MP, and was Head of the Prime Minister's Strategic Communications Unit between 2001 and 2003. He is author of *1 Out Of 10: From Downing Street Vision to Classroom Reality*.

Dennis Kavanagh is Emeritus Professor of Politics and Communications at Liverpool University. Before then he was Professor of Politics at Nottingham University. He is the author, co-author and editor of over 30 books. The most recent is (with Philip Cowley) *The British General Election of 2010*.

Lord Mandelson was a Cabinet minister in the governments headed by Tony Blair and Gordon Brown, a European Commissioner, Labour's director of campaigns and communications 1985–90 and MP for Hartlepool 1992–2004. He is the author of *The Third Man* (2010).

David Miliband is Labour MP for South Shields and was UK Foreign Secretary from 2007 to 2010.

James Purnell was Tony Blair's researcher from 1990 to 1992, and first met Philip Gould then. He subsequently worked in Downing Street between 1997 and 2001, when he was elected MP for Stalybridge and Hyde. He became Secretary of State for Culture, and for Work and Pensions, before standing down from Parliament in 2010. He is writing a book on *Britain's Fifty Year Plan*.

Introduction

Georgia Gould

Barely a week before my father died he took my sister and me back to Woking where he grew up. His was an ordinary suburban street; people were neither rich nor poor. They were working hard to provide for their children a better future than the life they'd had. These were the doors he'd knock on when he was 16, hearing time and time again how Labour, their party, had let them down, had ignored their aspirations and abandoned their values: opportunity, hard work and fairness as a reward for contribution. This was my father's heartland. I think the founders of New Labour came to the project in different ways: through the revisionist tradition in the Labour Party, the failure of the party to communicate beyond its base and the irrelevance of policy for the modern age. My father came to it here on the streets of Woking. He called it 'the land that Labour forgot'.

In all his years involved in politics this was his base. He was never happier than driving out of central London to Watford or Bromley, to a quiet suburban neighbourhood that mirrored that of his upbringing. It was here, in the thousands of focus groups, that he would test where the Labour Party was going, asking whether it was still the party of aspiration and of contribution.

Those focus groups were an experience – I and whoever else Dad had dragged along would sit in the corner subjected to the torrents of abuse which help the participants feel comfortable. These groups were his arena; his personality would flow through them: listening, challenging, even sometimes abandoning his professionalism entirely and getting into massive arguments.

He wouldn't accept people's surface views, would push them until he got to their core, their unconscious beliefs and prejudices.

He was aware that these might be at odds with their easily given opinions, but both counted. At first there was always an awkward, wary air, nervous laughter and hesitant answers, but I'd watch the participants gradually get caught up in the excitement, fighting to contribute. By the end, people seemed disappointed it was over, they almost seemed to glow – the effect of being listened to and of feeling their views really counted. I used to love the long journeys back discussing what it all meant, what long-term trajectories were hidden in those opinions.

Then he would sit and write up his notes. This wasn't a report, it was a strategy document with the flow of opinion at its heart. My father saw it as putting the voices of ordinary people at the heart of government. Even when what people said was difficult to hear and jarred on your values, about immigration or crime, he believed you had to listen. His motto was 'trust the people' and he never stopped believing that. In later years, as he saw a declining belief in politics, he argued for far greater engagement, a new participatory model of politics, and in his way it was to that he dedicated his career.

The ordering of my life has been through election campaigns. I remember the sting of 1992, when the death of my grandfather, combined with the bitter blow of losing that election, caused Dad to lock himself away in his office for months. Then came the excitement of 1997 – 'Things Can Only Get Better' playing on loop in our living room, waiting up until the early hours to see my parents come in, my Dad lifting me up glowing 'We did it'. In 2001 I stayed up all night at Millbank and will never forget walking out the next clear crisp morning, 'Lifted' by the Lighthouse Family playing in the background, into another four years of a Labour government. In 2005 I was a Labour Party Organiser in Mitcham and Morden and Dad and I would meet late at night or in the early hours discussing the twists and turns of the campaign. By 2010 I was a candidate in the local elections and my father spent election day out canvassing in Kentish Town. He was a terrible canvasser, using his focus group techniques to have long, deep conversations on the doorsteps interrupted constantly by phone calls checking the latest exit polls, but I was glad he was there.

He was many things – a campaigner, a pollster, a consultant. But the fundamental misunderstanding people sometimes have about what he did was that he was only about rebranding. He believed that to genuinely change perceptions, you needed to change the fundamentals – communication is about substance.

So at heart he was a strategist, a thinker. He would disappear inside his head for days, deconstructing an idea, then he'd sit and write a note putting it all down. He and Alastair Campbell often repeated, 'It's not a strategy unless its written down.' His notes fill his office, our cupboards and a vast storage unit. This was his goldmine – ideas.

His values were at his core. Brought up by two teachers, his mum a Dutch idealist, his father driven by his public service duty, my father always saw personal values and public values as synonymous. He believed every decision was a moral one and would agonise over which decision took precedence morally. He fought hard to keep his integrity and never wanted a formal role, all too aware of the compromises of office. He wanted to stay slightly on the outside and was more comfortable with that.

He was a total obsessive. He did everything frantically, couldn't talk on the phone without pacing constantly. He would often get lost in his ideas and typically would hang up halfway through a conversation or lose his passport between check-in and the plane.

He was full of contradictions, perfectly capable of giving you one piece of advice one day, the opposite the next, and in a way being right about both. The basis for my father's understanding of strategy was Hegelian, a sequence of action and reaction that never ends. My mother described this light bulb moment when he first discovered Hegel's dialect; often represented as a triad of thesis, antithesis and synthesis, as a student at the LSE in 1975. It was how he saw the flow of politics and strategy.

Although he was tribal about Labour, he never let dogma hold back his thinking, and would relentlessly examine every question from the point of first principles. He believed in depth and was constantly reading, seeking to ground his thinking in history. But, at the same time, he thought you needed flexibility for the modern world, to be able to continuously adapt for changing times. He believed you had to listen to the people, but that people respected and required leadership. For my father, strategy had to be constantly evolving to meet the demands of a rapidly changing landscape but, at the same time, it had to stick concretely to its grounding principles.

His genius came in handling competing ideas and finding a synthesis. New Labour at its heart was a mass of contradicting ideas: globalisation and community, compassion and toughness, fairness and responsibility. The third way was a synthesis or a compromise depending on your perspective.

One of his great gifts was his relentless optimism. He could find meaning in every failure or setback. He was the best person to call in a crisis as he would instantly have a multitude of potential strategies and could always see a path through. I remember my sister, minutes away from giving a big speech at our school's founder's day, discovering someone had locked away her bag containing the speech. All of us descended into panic but my Dad very calmly pulled out a copy from his pocket saying 'You always carry a spare copy of a speech.'

He wasn't perfect, of course, and he didn't expect perfection in others. He had time for people; he mentored a countless stream of friends and had a gift for helping them find meaning and purpose in their lives. He saw the best in people and I'm not sure I ever saw him give up on anyone. He could lift any situation, find humour in anything and put any problem in perspective. He'd say that everything would be all right, and you would always believe him.

Where did he sit in the New Labour family? I think he was often the bridge or the gel that held different groups together. His home was the party. I remember one summer working at the Labour Party headquarters and witnessing the energy he used to bring by just walking into the room. He loved the party, the buzz of the staff, the long-time servers. He was always able to provide a link between the party and the Leader's Office, and in the latter years he was able to provide a bridge between the Brownite and Blairite camps.

The New Labour project was the great purpose of my father's life. The huge figures of my childhood were Alastair Campbell, Peter Mandelson, Tony Blair and Gordon Brown. The early days of New Labour were golden times with a shared sense of project and purpose. And for all the ups and downs over the years, my father stayed close to all of them. Of course, eventually the project faltered, Labour lost again, the team went their separate ways. For him it was inevitable and he saw it as part of the bigger arc of history. He believed that the way New Labour changed Britain had had an enormous impact and shaped what came after. He saw it as the task of the next generation to renew the project again, adapted for a different context but part of the same thread.

This book was commissioned by Dennis Kavanagh, an old friend of my father, with whom he discussed politics for over 25 years. He wanted to explore my father's legacy on polling, strategy and the wider arena of politics. They discussed the book before he died. Dad was characteristically delighted by the idea so as a family we are very grateful to Dennis and all the contributors for making it happen.

In a way my Dad's greatest impact was not his political purpose but his personal one. In 2008 he was diagnosed with cancer while I was doing my finals at university. He was told he had a 50 per cent chance of survival, and the world caved in around me.

Thus began a four-year journey, of chemotherapy, radiotherapy and operations, taking us from New York to Newcastle. Naturally, he treated it as a campaign, constantly strategising. And he changed. He became calmer, more introspective and more confident. Somehow he learnt what was really important. When the cancer came back in 2010, I remember Dad, after a conversation with Tony Blair, saying that the cancer hadn't pushed him far enough, that he had more to learn.

He was still doing politics right until the end. He had a constant flow of political visitors and he said talking politics was the most effective distraction from the pain he was in. We worked together on an updated version of *The Unfinished Revolution*. It was crucial for him to get down on paper how much his political thinking had moved on from the early days.

His final campaign was the one we all have to face at some point, confronting death. He was a person of such optimism, courage and faith that hopelessness was never an option for him. So he found a way to empower himself. He ignored the general views on death and became determined to write about it, to give other families facing a terminal diagnosis hope and a different narrative on death. His book *When I Die: Lessons From the Death Zone*, published posthumously, is a story of how to grow, transform and live even when given a death sentence.

My father's death has left a massive hole in my life; there isn't a day I didn't speak to him, often up to three times, about life, football, politics. My life feels very empty without his constant interruptions.

We'd argue and debate politics constantly. My heartland is slightly different. It's in the ward I now represent in Camden where I see the lack of opportunities in some of our estates juxtaposed with the affluence of our leafier streets. It's the good state school I went to, where your background still defines your life chances. It's the alienation and lack of trust I see in some communities that I believe requires a total rethink about how we build a new social contract. So I have my own priorities, but we share the same core values. Dad would call it synthesis.

I think a lot about what he would say to those of us left behind, trying to carry on his life's campaign to see the Labour Party in office delivering on the values which he lived by.

He would tell us to never stop modernising, to understand that the future is defined by the past but also radically different. The coalition government has changed the landscape. If we answer yesterday's questions then we become moribund and our values die with us. People may agree or disagree with some aspects of the New Labour project but its core message, to never sit still, to constantly rethink and re-analyse, should always be at the heart of our thinking.

He would tell us to trust the people more than ever, to recognise that we are operating in a rapidly emptying stadium, and unless we genuinely engage with people at every level we will all become extinct.

He would tell us that integrity is everything in a fast moving, transparent world. That there is no longer any distinction between who we are personally and politically so we have to put values at the heart of everything we do.

He would tell us to understand the nature of globalisation but equally to understand the pressures it puts on local communities.

He would tell us to ignore conventional wisdom. By the time it's caught up, the world has moved on so you should follow your own judgement and do what you believe in.

He would tell us to never to give up. He worked on three election campaigns before he won one.

But most of all he would tell us to have a purpose, greater than any individual or personal ambition, to make that our lodestar and all else will follow. In his words – have faith and change the world. The point about the revolution is that it is never finished.

Philip Gould's Life and Work

Dennis Kavanagh

1

Philip Gould's death on 6 November 2011 at the age of 61 evoked a remarkable response. For over 30 years he had achieved some fame as a political strategist, probably the first self-described one in British politics, and one who played a crucial role in the development of New Labour and in the party's three general election victories between 1997 and 2005. Political figures across parties paid generous tributes to him. In his last months he had fought and movingly recorded in a series of newspaper articles and a television interview his losing battle with oesophageal cancer. The brave way he confronted death inspired other sufferers and brought his life and death to the attention of a much wider public.

Other chapters deal with various aspects of Philip's career. This one briefly outlines his life, discusses his use of focus groups, approach to political campaigns, relations with Labour leaders, political values and, finally, his achievements.

I first encountered Philip during the 1987 general election. He was outside Labour Party HQ in Walworth Rd, shouting into his mobile phone, competing with the roaring traffic, and gesticulating to summon a taxi. With his unruly mop of hair he seemed in some distress and the call seemed to matter a great deal. This was beginning of a 25-year friendship in which I talked to him regularly, particularly during general election campaigns. What follows draws on some of my conversations with him and a handful of the papers he provided.

Life

Philip Gould was born in 1950 in Beddington and grew up in Woking, near Surrey. A dyslexic, he failed the 11-plus, struggled at his secondary modern school and left with only one O Level. That background, as Georgia Gould notes in the introduction, grounded his politics. The young boy was already interested in election campaigns and joined Labour when he was 15, and as a teenager he loved canvassing and attending party meetings. By studying at night school he eventually made his way to Sussex University to read politics, and where he met his future wife Gail Rebuck. He studied for a Master's degree at the London School of Economics and then worked for a time in advertising. Following further study at the London Business School he set up his consultancy, Philip Gould Associates, working from a small room in his home.

A turning point came in October 1985 when Peter Mandelson, Labour's new communications director, asked him to conduct an audit of the party's communications. As Mandelson describes in his chapter, the report led him to ask Gould and Deborah Mattinson to manage Labour's polling and media strategy for the 1987 general election. Helping Labour to win elections was to be his vocation for the rest of his life. He was involved in setting up the Shadow Communications Agency (SCA) of Labour sympathisers in the PR and advertising industries who gave their services to the party for free. The election campaign won plaudits for its slick communications, but Labour still lost heavily. By now there was a familiar litany of adjectives whenever his name was mentioned – obsessive, driven, excitable, visionary, over the top, panicky and dishevelled

The prospects for 1992, with some changed party policies, SCA given more scope and a damaged Conservative government, looked more promising. But after Labour's defeat in the 1992 general election, the fourth in succession, there was a savage party reaction against the agency, and against Gould and Patricia Hewitt in particular, who had been prominent in the campaign. The attacks were led by party officials, members of the NEC and shadow ministers who, collectively, complained that their views had been marginalised by what John Prescott castigated as 'the beautiful people' from public relations and polling, including Mandelson and Gould. The SCA was disbanded.

His experience in Little Rock, Arkansas, working on the Bill Clinton campaign in October 1992 restored his self-confidence. There were many similarities to the recent British election. Labour's dismal record was matched by the Democrats' losing five of the six previous presidential elections. But in November Clinton showed that a party of the centre-left, running as 'new' Democrats, could win against a negative campaign of a right-wing incumbent.

Many in the Labour Party gave Gould's advocacy of so-called 'Clintonisation' a mixed reception. He wrote against the left's 'sneering' about Clinton in a *New Statesman* article, 'The American Dream'.[1] But the modernisers were in the cold as long as John Smith was leader, and Gould went off to work for the European Socialist parties. More significant was that the young Gordon Brown and Tony Blair had visited the Clinton team and they were coming to the same conclusions as Gould.

Another turning point was the election of Blair as party leader in July 1994. He, Mandelson and Campbell were part of an inner circle around Blair and Gordon Brown which plotted to modernise the Labour Party and end its run of election defeats.

The lessons he learned in Little Rock and applied to Labour's landslide election victory in 1997 were laid out in his book, *The Unfinished Revolution*. They were his core principles of modern campaigning: occupy the centre ground; appeal to the working middle class; rapid rebuttal of Opposition claims; win trust on the economy; concede, when wrong, and move on; and convey a clear sense of direction. The book became the bible of modern campaigning. An updated *Unfinished Revolution*, with a foreword by Blair, was published shortly before Gould's death.

During Labour's 13 years in government he was a key figure in Labour's campaigns, particularly 2001 and 2005, less so in 2010, and in the continuing communications strategies. He attended meetings in Number 10 four or five times a week, further meetings with other ministers and in party HQ, and conducted groups and wrote countless memos. When the memos leaked and there was media frenzy about the latest 'crisis', Blair told him to carry on writing them.

He was immensely pleased to be made a life peer in 2004. He had never held political office and regarded it as a reward for his years of service to the party. But the Lords soon lost its attraction for him, although a few weeks before he died he had attended the Lords to vote against the government's health bill. At the 2008 party conference Gordon Brown and Harriet Harman presented him with a special service award. Away from politics Gould worked with Freud Communications. He had worked on projects for the company since 2001 before becoming Deputy Chair, signing a contract after his cancer had been diagnosed. He mentored young members of staff and handled the account of its largest client, Mars. In a message to staff, announcing Philip's death, the chairman, Matthew Freud, wrote that the company was Philip's 'other family' and acknowledged how his influence 'is indelibly stamped on our philosophy, our values and our strategy'.

His cancer was diagnosed in January 2008. He prepared for his first operation like a champion athlete entering a big race, following a regime of exercise, dieting and meditation. He described his losing battle with the disease in a series of *Times* newspaper articles in 2011 when he was in what he called 'the death zone'. He approached this battle like one of his election campaigns; he made his peace with friends and foes and planned the details of the church service ('there will be no concessions to modernity', he warned) and the interment.

Facing death with bravery and dignity was his final project and, given its impact on the public, perhaps his most successful. He visited his planned burial plot in Highgate Cemetery and said 'I am going to be happy here'. A High Anglican (he converted while ill), his funeral on 15 November was a Requiem High Mass at All Saints in central London. The readings were given by Tony Blair and Gordon Brown, lessons by his daughters Grace and Georgia, and Alastair Campbell read the letter he had written to Gould the day before he died.

Philip's book on his illness and preparing for death, on which he worked until his final hours (dictating to his wife Gail), was published posthumously in April 2012 as *When I Die: Lessons from the Death Zone.*

Politics

Gould always believed that Labour was about providing people with a fair deal, 'helping the underdog', the kind of sentiments expressed by one of his favourite authors, George Orwell. He spoke for the people he grew up with in the Woking suburbs, the working class and lower middle class, living 'lives of struggle and hard work' who aspired to better things. He wrote that 'the old working-class was becoming a new middle-class: aspiring, consuming, choosing what was best for themselves and their families ... I knew this, because they were my life.' Many of them had lost faith with Labour in the 1970s and 1980s. He quoted an overseas observer of the reactions of one of his focus groups in Putney 1997: 'what did you do to these people that they fear you so much'.

Because he was a key figure in the project of Labour breaking with its immediate and electorally damaging past, he was criticised by the left for helping the party to abandon its core values. This accusation is inaccurate. Although a Labour loyalist and advocate of active government, state provision of education and health, and redistribution, he knew the party had to adapt to changing times. For him the New Labour project was always progressive. But like other modernisers he said Labour had to take account of a changed world, of globalisation, the 24/7 media, and citizens expecting more personal services and greater value for money. He was scarred by the effectiveness of the Tory campaign in 1992 which painted Labour as an untrustworthy tax-spend party. Never again should the party give the Conservatives an opportunity of translating Labour's spending pledges into rises in income tax; hence Gordon Brown's election pledge in 1997 not to increase taxes and to keep to tight Conservative spending plans. Over the years he regularly warned the party about voters' concerns about crime, immigration, illegal asylum and welfare scroungers.

Resentment over immigration and asylum had less to do with race than with the voters' sense of unfairness. Analysis of how these issues damaged Labour in 2010 show he was ahead of the curve. He was reporting the perceptions of voters, something at times forgotten by critics.

He was a Blairite insofar as he accepted Blair's ideas of liberal intervention abroad and the Iraq war, though not the aftermath, and supported Blair's public service reform agenda, calling it 'right on every level'.[2] Patricia Hewitt claims that he was the first to use the term 'New Labour' in a note in 1989 (I had always credited the term to her). But in his last months he thought that the New Labour project needed new answers to the problems of equality, poverty and tax and that any answers would be heavily social democratic.

Before New Labour

Gould always had to contend with the fact that for some years much of the Labour Party was resistant to modern communication methods and the idea of studying the mood of the electorate. Such suggestions seemed to fly in the face of the party's leadership role. Following the party's third successive election defeat in 1959, the NEC refused pleas to provide funds for a survey into the reasons for the defeat. The path-breaking *Must Labour Lose* survey (1960) was financed privately.[3] The book gave ample warnings about the aspirations of the working class, not least for home ownership, the unpopularity of the unions and nationalisation and that Labour was seen as the party for the poor and the old. Thirty years later, similar warnings were being made by Gould and by Giles Radice's *Southern Discomfort*.[4] Only in 1968 did the NEC vote a modest sum for polling. MORI, the party's pollster for all general elections between February 1974 and 1987, regularly had to struggle for a budget.

Part of the problem lay in the party's structure. The annual conference, and the NEC elected by conference, was the voice of the activists and the trade unions. At times James Callaghan and

Neil Kinnock found themselves in the minority on the NEC. One party treasurer, Aneurin Bevan, condemned polls for taking the poetry out of politics. By 1970 a successor as party treasurer, the left-wing Norman Atkinson, opposed opinion polling, boasting that if he wanted to know the views of voters he would consult 20 of his party activists. The prevalent view of such people was that Labour needed only to 'get out the vote'.

Another problem was that when the party was divided between left and right, the findings of private opinion polls could become a victim of internal faction fighting. Many of the findings were depressing for left-wing policy advocates.

After the fourth successive election defeat, in 1992, Gould realised that campaigning, however brilliant, was not enough to offset the problems facing Labour. The party structure and culture would have to change if it were to win power again. Within days of the election he wrote me an eleven-page letter. Among the reasons why Labour lost, he mentioned:

1. Party affinity, the sense that 'a political party is for me' and Labour was losing out as people became more upmarket and aspirational.
2. The price of voting Labour; paying more taxes and interest rates will increase.
3. The changing nature of the voting decision; it was becoming more instrumental (what is good for me and my family) and less ideological.
4. The failure to erode Labour's deficits on leadership and the economy.
5. The effect of the tabloid press.
6. The clarity of the centre-right message and the lack of a clear left message.
7. The lack of organisational homogeneity; the party was one thing at the top, but less so at the bottom.
8. The need for the party organisation to adapt more quickly than ever before.

He was not able to act on this post mortem because he was in the wilderness. He thought he was finished as a Labour strategist, ending his letter that he hoped he would 'not be discussing another defeat after another excellent campaign in June 1996. Somehow, for all sorts of reasons I doubt it.'

Despite his despair about his own role, one can already discern the germ of the changes later made to the party under Blair and some of the orienting ideas of New Labour.

Campaigning

Gould loved election campaigns, writing of them in the revised edition of his book as 'a noble thing, complete in itself, not a pathway to something else'.[5] He approached them like grand projects. They made his adrenalin flow, as he worked 18-hour days, conducting groups, writing reports, attending meetings and arguing passionately about what should be done. Everything was urgent: time was short: the campaign was a 'surrogate war'.

Colleagues and rivals acknowledged he was always rethinking and learning. In elections in 1986, 1987 and 1992, in Britain and in the United States, negative campaigning seemed to be the rage as Conservatives and Republicans successfully exploited fear – fear about tax, about defence and, in Britain, about Europe. His experience working for Labour in 1987 and 1992 showed him that good communications could take Labour only so far. They could not compensate for weaknesses on leadership, the economy, and trust. Good communications had to be aligned with good policy. But his main concern was with getting everything ready for the campaign, understandable after so many defeats.

In 1997 and 2001 Labour fought what he called total or permanent campaigns, catering for the 24/7 media. He recommended the book *The New Prince* by Clinton's pollster, Dick Morris.[6] Controversially, it argued that for the President (and by extension the Prime Minister) every day was akin to an election day; and strength came from being popular and ahead in the opinion polls. For the critics, alarmed by Labour's spin and media management, this approach smacked of populism and continuous campaigning rather than governing. He used to comment in the course of a campaign, 'We won that day and we won the week.' It helped that Blair had already achieved what Gould had recommended: central command of the party, to give him control of the party message.

But after 2001 Gould abandoned this stance. In the papers 'The Not So Permanent Campaign' (2002) and 'The Empty Stadium' (2003), written with Douglas Alexander, he recanted. He likened politicians to footballers playing in empty stadiums; the spectators had lost interest and gone home. Similarly, the permanent campaign was a producer-dominated model that turned people off and was reflected in slumps in voting turnout and then in the decline in party membership.

If voters were to be engaged, they expected to be heard and politicians to be more accountable to them. They were empowered as consumers and looked for the same in politics; they wanted to be in the driving seat. Politicians had to be more open and seek permission to speak in an age of the internet, text messaging, phone-ins, debates and focus groups.

A regular theme of Gould's advice to Labour leaders was the importance of change. In a lengthy memo to Blair on 17 May 1994, he advised Blair to embrace the strategy of change.

The prose was high-flown:

Change is a complete political project that meets the mood, and seizes the mood.

Again, change is a new approach to politics, and a political leader that embodies that approach. It is about radical ideas and fresh new solutions; it is about excitement and momentum; it is about practical, sensible policies, but it is also about vision and hope. Above all it is about leadership that articulates the need for change and gives the electorate the confidence to make the change.

This is the heart of the modernising project.

More than a decade later, in a memo to Gordon Brown, dated 21 February 2005, Gould assured him he was certain to take over and become leader, and that he would support him. But he warned Brown he would have to embrace change.

> Already around 60% of the voters want dramatic change. This mood for change is not rational: it is a distinctive sense that after 8 or 12 years that is long enough in power. This will be a key dynamic for the next election campaign.
>
> You have to completely meet this mood for change. You have to represents renewal, change, a fresh start ... You are the change that Britain needs.

The memos of course said little about the direction of change and little about the necessary policies.

Focus Groups

Gould was hardly the first to use focus groups in politics. They were developed in the United States and employed by Tim Bell at Saatchi & Saatchi for the Conservatives before the 1979 general election. But nobody had employed them so systematically and made them so influential for a party before Gould. Such groups consist of ten or so individuals. He selected target voters, often former Labour or non-voters in a marginal seat. They were obviously not representative of a wider public, but of a target group. As the moderator he decided the questions, tested reactions to themes and slogans and films and pictures. His approach was highly interventionist and he could be quite brutal in guiding the discussion and cutting people off. The point of the meetings was to enable him to write his report and to craft the 'message'. During election campaigns he would conduct groups during an evening and write his report late at night for Blair.

Putting his thoughts on paper was crucial; if it was not written down it did not exist. Gould's reports were unmistakeable. They were well spaced out, using bullet points, heavy type, and expressed in an uncompromising, colourful language. They were always constructive; even when he was claiming that the party's position was dire he would have practical suggestions for turning it round. A flavour of his work can be seen in a focus group report and conclusions on 3 June 2009, based on a number of groups and published and unpublished polling: 'The personal mood of the group was flat but not universally despondent.'

On the Labour Party, feeling was 'More negative than for any time in 20 years ... It was impossible to get one respondent to say one positive thing about the government.'

On leadership, he wrote: 'Views of Gordon Brown are if anything more negative than views of Labour. The starting point is his absence of a mandate – "ignorant", "scruffy", "weak", "hopeless".'

After reviewing options for Labour to recover, Gould concluded:

> We have not fully and conclusively lost the electorate...But the political space can still be found where we can advance, and the public will in the right circumstances be prepared to hear us again. All is not yet lost.

Focus groups are not without their critics. An academic complained that 'reactions are likely to be multiple, disparate, inconsistent and sometimes confused'.[7] Within the party there were complaints that the groups were responding to a right-wing, *Daily Mail*-driven agenda. Other critics complained that the groups were denuding politics of convictions and ideology.

His former business partner, Deborah Mattinson, agrees that focus groups are no substitute for a politician being authentic. But she adds that moving Labour from 'beyond the pale' in the 1980s 'to being the people's politicians in 1997 could not have been achieved without the insights and advice from members of the public' derived from the groups.[8] Gould believed groups were a positive phenomenon for politics, rarely doubting that he was hearing what people thought. He was, he wrote in the revised edition of his book, 'most happy and fulfilled conducting focus groups'.[9] To those who argued that government by groups was the abdication of leadership, he countered that politicians had a duty to listen, and that people were entitled to have a voice in shaping the policies that affected them and not receive them from on high. He thought there was no substitute for talking directly to voters

Leaders

Strategists and pollsters are employed by political parties. But if British politics is not presidential, personal leadership has become a major factor, an electoral asset or handicap for the party. The modern media coverage of politics and the emphasis on person-alisation makes the leader the chief carrier of the party's message. But Gould was intrigued by what he called a leader's charisma, an indefinable quality that attracted voters. One either had it or one did not. And Blair had it.

Previous pollsters had tried and failed to establish a close relationship with the party leader. For both the Labour and Conservative parties the pollster was below stairs; the poll findings were usually mediated by the leader's aides and senior party officials. That Gould was the first pollster who could go directly to the leader was a measure of Blair's dominance and the changes in the Labour Party. Previous pollsters must have envied his continuous access.

With Neil Kinnock there was no close relationship, although he admired Kinnock's efforts to reform the party. Opinion polling was done by MORI and Gould coordinated the work of the SCA. But the public perception of Kinnock's leadership was an elephant in the room. The party's weakness on leadership was not discussed in front of the party leader, but all were aware of the downside.

John Smith had not battled for modernisation but had rather watched as Neil Kinnock battled. Gould admitted that Smith, as shadow chancellor, froze him out before and, as party leader, after the 1992 election. He was angry that Gould argued against his proposals for increasing taxes and uprating child benefits and pensions. Gould was warned by Smith's advisers to give him a wide berth. Smith had little time for polling and public relations. The modernisers dispersed. Gould went off to work for the European

Socialists during 1993 and early 1994. Patricia Hewitt went to the IPPR and Peter Mandelson had become an MP. The project of modernising Labour seemed to be still-born.

Gould readily accepted he was a Blairite but his loyalty above all was to the party, with or without Blair His admiration for Blair and respect for him personally deepened over time. His appreciation for what he called Blair's 'political genius' increased further as he observed how Brown handled the job of leadership. He did not claim to influence Blair because he thought the leader already 'had an intuitive grasp of public opinion'. The admiration was reciprocated. After his death Blair said that Gould 'was my guide and mentor'. Gould delivered some tough messages to Blair, telling him in leaked memos in 2000 that he was perceived as 'all spin and no substance' and 'lacks conviction'. He recognised Gordon Brown as the rightful successor and worked for a smooth transition in late 2005 early 2006. He could give Blair bad news without a problem, but could not do the same for Gordon Brown because Gould felt he became angry and depressed.

He thought Brown's gifts outweighed his deficiencies until he was Prime Minister. There had been some mistrust between the two since Gould had backed Tony Blair over Brown for the party leadership in 1994. Brown suspected that Gould's polling and focus group reports to Blair were biased. In particular, he resented Gould's claims that there was public opposition to the idea of a higher tax rate for those earning salaries over £100,000 annually, a step Brown favoured. In 1996 Brown decided he wanted his own pollster and recruited Deborah Mattinson. (Disappointingly for him, her research supported Gould's findings.) For long Gould treated the two men as near equals, but giving Blair reports of his groups a few minutes before Brown during general elections.

Gould acknowledged Brown's strengths and, with Campbell, worked to force an unwilling Blair to bring Brown to play a central role in the 2005 general election campaign, at one point reminding Blair that Brown was more of an electoral asset than he. In the transition talks following that general election, he and Campbell were members of 'Team Blair'. Brown and Blair, accompanied by their aides, were like rival mobsters accompanied by their protective groups of minders negotiating how to divide the spoils. Gould also thought that Blair should make clear early after 2005 that he would be standing down in the course of the Parliament.

For all the talk among Brown's admirers of his moral compass, Gould had doubts about his character. He was appalled at Brown's treatment of colleagues and the attempted coup in September 2006. He could not stand being in the same room as some of Brown's associates. But he hoped Brown might overcome his deficiencies once he had achieved his ambition of being Prime Minister.

After 2005 he knew that the party would have to renew itself after being in power for over eight years and had occasional doubts that Brown was the man for the task: was he still New Labour? Had he run out of ideas? In a note dated 20 August 2006, he wrote to Brown saying that if he became leader the party had an opportunity if it renewed itself. But there should be a contest, which would be an important step in legitimising Brown's leadership:

> A top down hand-over will feel undemocratic and undermine the chance of renewal. There needs to be rite of passage into the new leadership.

It was not to be, and Gould felt increasingly over time that the absence of a contested election compromised Brown from the beginning.

He regularly suggested that Brown should call a general election soon after becoming leader. The action, he claimed, would transform perceptions of Brown. He would be seen as decisive and courageous, and determined to seek his own mandate. In a note to Brown dated 2 February 2005, he wrote:

> I believe the best way of achieving this 'improvement of our vote' is to hold an early election after a short period of intense and compelling activity ... you need to build on this and translate it into a new mandate. I am sure that this strategy will work.

He effectively gave up on Brown after his failure to call an election in October 2007. He thought there was no way back for the party as long as Brown was leader. In 2009, after James Purnell's resignation, he was disappointed that David Miliband did not resign from the Cabinet and challenge Brown for the leadership. In time he came to accept Miliband's reasons for not standing but felt that he had missed his big opportunity. Despite the distrust among some Brown aides, he worked with total commitment on the 2010 election campaign and thought that with a different leader the party would have added 2–3 per cent to its share of vote and opened the way for Labour to form a coalition. He regarded the failure of the Conservatives to gain a winning majority as one of the most rewarding campaigns he had been involved in.

In 2010, despite his returning cancer and diminishing energy, he worked for David Miliband in the leadership contest while expecting Ed to win on a second ballot. He had good relations with Ed and spoke to him nightly during the general election campaign. But he regarded the outcome as a disaster for both him and the party. He regarded David as a complete article and Ed as a work still in progress. Ed's pitch during the leadership campaign was that he was not New Labour, letting it be known that he wanted to eradicate New Labour, just as Blair had defined his early leadership by wanting to abolish Clause IV.

Shortly before his death, Gould was wondering if Labour should be looking to a new generation for political leadership. The present one might be too much defined and infected by the Blair–Brown rivalry. He was confident, however, that the decency of the Miliband brothers would preclude the damage done to the party by the Blair–Brown battles.

For all his leaked memos and his self-revelatory *Unfinished Revolution*, Gould was a private person. He had no desk in Number 10, never held political office or thought of running for one, although he took delight in his daughter's election as a Labour councillor. He was disappointed at the kiss-and-tell instant memoirs of Labour politicians. He kept detailed notes and diaries of his experiences at the heart of New Labour but had no intention of publishing them in his lifetime. He appreciated Brown's visits and sympathy in his final weeks and did not want to publish anything hurtful. He considered it a breach of trust for Kinnock's aides to allow the playwright David Hare the access for his play *The Absence of War* and Blair's decision to allow similar access to the writer Robert Harris to write about the last days of the 1997 general election campaign.

Because he never held an office or had a desk in Number 10, Gould always knew that he had to wait to be called. It was another reason why he had to write his notes. As already noted, Labour's defeat in the 1992 election affected him profoundly and he was a casualty in the backlash against the party's election campaign. In vain did some point out that Labour's problem was the product and not its presentation. But there was also simmering resentment of Gould on the left and the old right who thought that the work of New Labour meant the party was losing its soul. Such critics complained the party's message and policies were being tailored to a sector of the electorate whose views were shaped by a right-wing press.

When some of Gould's memos to Blair were leaked, the commentariat exploded. A May 2000 memo told Blair that 'TB is not believed to be real' and 'TB is out of touch, he does not care.' The *Guardian*'s Hugo Young complained that, with Labour leading in the Gallup poll by 16 points, these criticisms were 'causing self-destructive alarm' and Gould's remedies were waffle. Young continued:

> his is the politics, essentially, of cowardice, offending no one, challenging nobody, voicing not the conviction of a true prophet but the half-perceived prejudices of the masses before whom he stands transfixed.[10]

On the same day a *Times* editorial thought that Gould's advice was the opposite of leadership and that Tony Blair 'should inform Mr Gould that advice based on these assumptions is not worth sending'. Twelve years later, an editorial written soon after his funeral praised him as 'a remarkable man' and 'a clear-eyed realist, determined to see the world as it is and force others to do so. Realist and romantic, a most unusual combination.'[11]

Gould's Contribution to British Politics

Philip was one of the Labour figures who helped to shift the political agenda. If Labour had gradually come to accept some of Margaret Thatcher's policies, in his words 'conceding and moving on', the Conservatives had to do the same after a decade of New Labour – constitutional change, the minimum wage, Bank of England independence, a changed political culture, and investment in public services and public service reform. By 2010 all major parties were in favour of the goals of social justice and economic efficiency.

He played an important role in the adoption of modern campaign tools – rebuttal, a war room, 24/7 campaigning, winning trust on the economy and occupying the centre ground. After 2001, however, he backed away from some elements of the permanent campaign. Many of these features were borrowed wholesale by the young Conservative modernisers around David Cameron and George Osborne.

He was an early advocate of the need for Labour to change radically, indeed to become New Labour; he had tried and failed to persuade Kinnock to use the term in a speech. After the defeat in 1992, he thought the party would have to change from top to bottom and become an electoral professional political party. Some important changes had begun under Kinnock – shorter lines of communication, an abandonment of some vote-losing policies, and a stronger leader's office. Reform was carried further under Blair. A Gould memo, written in 1995, calling for replacing the party's competing and overlapping structures with a single line of command, leading to Mr Blair; central control of communications; and a new campaign structure with a war room, was largely acted on for the 1997 election.

Some (notably Matthew d'Ancona) claim Gould helped to transform not one party but two, including the Conservatives.

That is true of the young modernisers (as shown in their chapters, Andrew Cooper and Danny Finkelstein did so from a very early point) around Cameron and Osborne, with their project of decontaminating the party's brand, but is less true of the rest of the party below. When William Hague in 1999 gave each member of his shadow team a copy of *The Unfinished Revolution* inscribed with the words: 'Know thine enemy', his purpose was not to learn from Labour's 1997 success but how to defeat Labour. A later leader, Michael Howard, told his colleagues who said they had read the book 'then read it again', and invited young Steve Hilton to be 'my Philip Gould'. But such efforts at modernisation were only half-hearted until Cameron came along. As Andrew Cooper notes, Gould thought Cameron was the first Tory leader to 'get it'.

Gould pioneered the idea of the political strategist, one who monitored public opinion, shaped the campaign strategy and had a close relationship with the party leader. MORI's Bob Worcester came close to this position under Harold Wilson, but his contributions were always mediated by the NEC and staff in the leader's office. Gould's closeness and importance to the leader was akin to an American presidential pollster. Since 2011, a pollster has a formal position in 10 Downing Street. Indeed, Andrew Cooper's appointment to Number 10 as his political strategist, the first pollster to have such a position, is Cameron's attempt to emulate, in-house, Gould's role under Blair.

He did more than anybody to emphasise the importance in election campaigns of focus groups. Gould's experience in 1992 confirmed his faith in these groups. He always doubted the Labour leads reported in the quantitative polls because his groups showed a lack of enthusiasm and doubts about the party leadership and economic policy. But the findings of the groups were not a stand-alone item. He used them to deliver punchy practical notes on what the party should do in its communications to address voters' concerns.

Philip was fascinated with change. He said a permanent revolution in government would take over from permanent campaigning. It is appropriate that his great book was entitled

The Unfinished Revolution. Almost the last words of the revised edition, knowing that he was near death, were addressed to the next generation:

> I believe that there is never a time when the revolution is finished, never a time to stop thinking, to stop renewing, to stop trying to change the world if only by a little.[12]

Notes

1. Philip Gould, 'The American Dream', *New Statesman*, 15 January 1993.
2. Philip Gould, *The Unfinished Revolution* (Little, Brown, 2011), p. 491.
3. Mark Abrams and Richard Rose, *Must Labour Lose* (Penguin, 1960).
4. Giles Radice, *Southern Discomfort* (Fabian Society, 1992).
5. Gould, *Unfinished Revolution*, p. 471.
6. Dick Morris, *The New Prince* (Renaissance Books, 1999).
7. Richard Rose, *The Prime Minister in a Shrinking World* (Polity, 2001), p. 222.
8. Deborah Mattinson, *Talking to a Brick Wall* (Biteback, 2010), p. 105.
9. Gould, *Unfinished Revolution*, p. 416.
10. Hugo Young, 'The leaks show whose head must roll. That of Gould', *Guardian*, 20 July 2000.
11. 'The Optimist', *The Times*, 8 November 2011.
12. Gould, *Unfinished Revolution*, p. 540.

Friendship in Politics

Alastair Campbell

2

A few days after Philip died, my partner Fiona asked me what I found myself remembering more: Philip the political colleague or Philip the personal friend? I took a few moments to allow snapshots and images to flood into my mind ... Philip announcing his presence in Labour election campaign HQ, coat and briefcase flapping, thought for the day emerging from his mouth, before spilling his vitamin pills all over my desk; Philip at a football match missing a goal because he was texting the *Sunday Times* trying to get an early shout on their poll figures; Philip phoning just before midnight from Huddersfield or Watford or Oldham or Corby to tell me how the focus groups had gone; Philip juggling huge quantities of meat on a holiday barbecue whilst setting out where he felt New Labour was going right, and where we were going wrong; Philip sitting down to tell Tony Blair that the speech he was due to deliver in a few hours had 'lost the plot'; Philip working with me to try to get Tony and Gordon Brown working together better; Philip failing to pronounce French place-names, and not doing much better with quite a lot of English ones; Philip refusing to let me leave a restaurant on holiday until we have come up with a better strapline for the party conference; Philip in the back of the car we shared to work hundreds of times, the conversation careering from politics to sport, work to family, serious to funny ... I found myself replying to Fiona: 'I find them inseparable, Philip the colleague and Philip the friend.' Some of the most political moments in our relationship came when we were on holiday. Some of the greatest acts of friendship, and the smallest touches of kindness, came as we were struggling to hold a campaign together, or dealing with a political storm. We were team-mates, but as a result became close friends. For both of us, teamship was a vital part of any major project, and the campaign a place where genuine friendship could be formed.

It was Harry Truman who said 'if you want a friend in Washington, get a dog', and it was a phrase my mother-in-law would remind me of from time to time whenever she felt I was getting an unfair hammering in the press, and could sense one or two of 'our own people' stoking the fires a little. But if by his paean to canine companionship Truman meant that there was no such thing as friendship in politics, then I think he was very wrong. If Truman were around to make his case, then I am not the only one who would call Philip Gould as the first witness for the defence that friendship in politics is not only possible, but real, and essential for success. When I spoke at Philip's funeral, and looked around the packed church, I saw people from all stages and all parts of his life, who were genuine friends of his.

Of course there are enmities in politics, including on your own side. This is not the place to go into the exhaustively told story of difficulties in the relationships at the top of New Labour, which were real, and draining. Nor was Philip a saint. He had considerable powers of forgiveness, and prided himself on always keeping bridges open even to adversaries others might find beyond the pale, but he had enemies too, or at least people for whom he had little time, trust or respect because all they brought to the table was negativity and the undermining of others. Even with them, however, he would want to look for redeeming features, involve them, try through openness and candour to bring them back closer into the fold. The desire to be positive almost always beat the desire to be negative when it came to Philip's assessment of people, and his view of strategy. He had enormous energy, drive, and capacity for love, and he put it to good use.

There are many ways to judge people you know. Two important ones for me are how they relate to my children, and what their own children are like. Georgia and Grace are wonderful young women who are a tribute to a mother and father who always led busy lives, but who were always utterly devoted to their daughters. As for Philip's relationship with my own children, they loved him for the fun, the joy, the support and the friendship he brought into our lives.

Tony Blair could never understand how Philip and I could spend so much time working together, then go on holiday together as well. Partly, of course, it was a way of carrying on working. We shared workaholic tendencies and we shared an obsession with doing all we could to help Labour win and, once we had won the first time, win again. Some of our best strategies, ideas, lines and slogans came from long holiday chats occasionally interrupted by Gail and Fiona asking if 'you two' ever had a conversation that didn't mention TB–GB. (answer not many, even to the end). But more than that he was just enormous fun to be with. Though all too often he created mayhem by losing passports or wallets or jackets (just as occasionally he would lose our entire election plans on a train coming back from one of his focus groups), he was the organiser, the originator of trips and tournaments, madcap events that turned inevitably into holiday highlights. And when times were tough, there was no better friend. Always loyal, but understanding that loyalty required honesty and frankness, and ideas about how to make things better.

His capacity for love embraced the Labour Party. When I say he loved the Labour Party, I do not just mean that he had an interest in its history, shared its basic values, felt deeply its power to do good for people too often left behind by the political and ruling elite. All that is true. But what I mean is that he loved the people who campaigned for it, breathed it day and night, worked for it. The strength of these feelings came from those he had as a child. Yes, he was into football and fishing and the stuff of many boys' childhoods. But he loved politics from the moment he first became aware of it. He reckoned he was six when he scribbled his first campaign thoughts, imagining himself as an adviser to Harold Wilson. He must also be the only ten-year-old ever to have pleaded with his parents to forgo a family holiday because he wanted to stay in front of the TV at home and watch the US Party Conventions.

If that suggests a political obsessive, then fair enough. Yet his was a politics always rooted in real people who were not political obsessives. He had a strong sense, not least through his parents, both teachers, of politics and public service being closely aligned. But he also sensed that for most people politics was something that happened to them, rather than something they felt they could influence and control. He felt that particularly disadvantaged the already disadvantaged, and that of the main parties, only Labour really cared about that. Equally strongly, however, he felt that during the Thatcher era, parts of the Labour Party forgot what it was for, and lost touch with the very people he believed we should be serving. New Labour was for him a return to the Labour Party he first believed in, and a return to power not just for the party but for the kind of people he grew up with. And though he liked the sense of closeness to power, friendship with two successive Prime Ministers, and the status that came with a seat in the House of Lords, those people he grew up with, and their values, were always dominant in his thinking. It is what led focus groups to become a part of the New Labour history.

Something close to mythology has now developed around Philip's focus groups. I was something of a late convert to them. Initially, they became just one more thing for the mutual mockery which was a part of our friendship. I felt he overstated the wisdom of the people he met, and overstated their importance to strategy, which I believed had to come through strong political instinct. In other words, I believed people were there to be led. He believed that if we really listened to them, we would learn things that helped leadership. What I learned over time is that the two approaches can coexist well. His mockery of me was often rooted in his observation that I was an obsessive whose obsessions came from whatever happened to be my bugbear at the time. The anti-jogger who later ran marathons. The technophobe who became a social media junkie. The focus group sceptic who became a focus group fan. It's why he was sure I would find God – 'from "we don't do God" to "why I now do God" – it's your next bestseller'. My conversion on focus groups came after sitting at the back and watching Philip conduct them. He really liked the people. He loved the detail of their lives, and his manner ensured they would be open and frank. He made them feel it was the most natural thing in the world to be sitting in a stranger's front room and talking about politics. I never once heard anyone ask him who he represented. He always started by saying he had done focus groups in places as varied as Jamaica and Belgium and America and that he was going to ask them to say something about their lives, then have a discussion about how and why they might vote at the next election. He always liked me to stay out of sight in case anyone recognised me. But every now and then it was impossible not to laugh out loud from behind the cupboard or the curtain where he had asked me to hide; as when he was doing a group in Watford, and as they explained one by one who they were, and a woman introduced herself as Jane, Philip interjected: 'my first girlfriend was called Jane ... she went on to kill herself'. What Jane was meant to make of this information was not entirely clear. But it gave us something to laugh about on the late-night drive home as we went over what they had said, and he began to write a note that would be on Tony's desk by the time he was up the following morning.

For some, focus groups were a symbol of the professionalisation and consumerisation of politics. For Philip, they were not just a tool of strategic development. They were a profoundly democratic way of ensuring that those voices forgotten in the bad old days were never forgotten by New Labour. They were a means by which people not normally consulted could get their voice heard. He never tired of doing them. Once I had seen their value, I never attended one without getting some kind of additional insight or thought that I could take back to TB. Philip did so on an industrial, systemic basis. Of course, politicians have their own contacts and experiences. But the reality is that being Prime Minister, as Tony Blair himself once said, is something of a conspiracy against normality. It is not possible, because of security, the workload, the nature of the position, to be 'in touch' in the same way as it is in Opposition. What Philip did was explore in depth what people were thinking and saying, and then make sense of that, strategically, for a leader who was always conscious of the difference between media opinion and public opinion, and wanted to know in depth where real public opinion lay.

When we made the transition from Opposition to government in 1997, Philip had no desire to move into Downing Street. He started to come in regularly almost by accident, bumping into Tony one day in a corridor, Tony realising we were missing some of his insight, and inviting him to the next Monday morning meeting. But he still didn't want a pass. He saw himself very much as the Labour Party man advising the Prime Minister and the government. He was interested in everything that was going on, and closely followed the policy debates as they developed. But part of his mind was distilling everything through the prism of what this meant for the party come the next election, and the next campaign. He loved election campaigns. But he knew that the successful ones required focus every day of every week of every year, and while we were busy with government, his mind was in there whirring away about the next campaign.

Campaigns are team games. If the driver of the bus isn't there, you don't have a campaign. You can design the best leaflet politics has ever seen. But if you don't have people to stick it through letter boxes, you might as well not bother. Philip's team was Labour. 'Pollster' doesn't really say the half of it. He was an integral member of the inner team that worked to get Labour back into power, and stay there for more than the usual single Parliament breathing space for the Tories. He was not a speechwriter but he was the most brilliant analyst of speech drafts. His notes on them always improved the final product. He was also great in a crisis, and always able to lift people and campaigns when they were low. He was that rare thing in politics – someone who was strategic, tactical and empathetic all in one. He was a rock.

Of course the leaders, and *the* leader in particular, are the most important people in a campaign, particularly in the media age. Every campaign will have a top table of strategists who will be trying to marry up the day to day, the frenzies and the mishaps, the threats and opportunities, with the agreed overall strategy for the campaign. But once that top table meeting has broken up, you need the systems and the people to turn the directions from the campaign leaders into action. For some top-table people, once the instructions are given, they see their job as done. But Philip understood the importance of every level of the campaign. He understood that at every level of the team you need team builders. People who will take it on themselves to think about the morale of others, the way people feel about the campaign, where they fit. One of the reasons Philip had so many friends is that that is the kind of role he always played. Keeping spirits up. Understanding that when things are tough is when the coolest heads and the ability to give a bit of lift are called for.

During a tough campaign you learn who you would happily be in the trenches with, who you would run through a brick wall for. Stuff happens. Things go wrong. People do and say things they shouldn't. Mistakes get made. At those times, the team player asks: what can I do to help? How can I act so that the damage from this is minimised? What can we do to support the person who screwed up? Is there any way of using this to get back on strategic track? These were questions that Philip rose to instinctively. Like the time our war book was leaked to the Tories, who were about to make a big song and dance of it at a press conference. I said we should publish it first, to show that we had a strategy and we were sticking to it. Most people were against the idea, and fussing about questions it was too late to answer, like how did it get out, who leaked it, what if this, what if that? Philip was with me and together we persuaded people we had to do it and we had to do it now. I would happily have run through a brick wall for Philip. And I know he would do the same for me.

Or like the day of what must surely be the most disastrous manifesto launch in election history. 2001. *Schools and Hospitals First* the rather prosaic slogan. The whole Cabinet heads to Birmingham. Tony leads the press conference. It all goes well. Then we visit a hospital, and a finger-wagging, TB-hectoring, NHS-attacking Sharon Storer enters the political lexicon. The manifesto barely gets a mention on the lunchtime news. Oh well, how did the song go? – Things can only get better? Not this time.

Next up, Home Secretary Jack Straw gets slow-handclapped at the Police Federation. That's a double whammy for the early evening news. By the 10 o'clock news, bliss and beauty has turned to heaven for journalists not too fussed about covering the finer points of policy on health and education, when John Prescott lands one of the most famous punches ever thrown outside a boxing ring.

Yes, that all happened in one single day, 16 May 2001, one of the most important days of the campaign. When we arrived at party HQ, heads were down, people were worried. Philip and I sat at our desks and loudly launched a competition to dream up ideas about what could go wrong next. By the time Philip was adding to the sweepstake Tony Blair's secret love child with Clare Short being revealed in the *News of the World*, the mood was lifting a little.

If there could be humour then, there was none on the day government weapons inspector David Kelly died. With the exception of the deaths of family and close friends, it was perhaps the worst day of my life, not merely for the tragedy that had taken place, but because of where I could sense it was heading. As I said in my diary, I felt like a juggernaut was coming my way. I got a lot of support from a lot of people. But there is a little six-word entry in my diary for that day that shows how Philip always goes the extra mile. 'Philip came round to the house.' He just appeared, knew how low I would be, knew how he would need to lift me, and he did.

Even when I did the London marathon, whilst my own family enjoyed the drama of the Mall and the free food and drink, Philip ventured out on the course, and he did a very good Woody Allen-Zelig impersonation, popping up all over the place to say 'come on, you can do it'.

And 'come on, you can do it' is pretty much what he said to the Labour Party ever since he started giving advice to Neil Kinnock. Though we lost on 6 May 2010, we won a lot on the way, and we did a lot of good along the way, and nobody should underestimate Philip's role in that. I know that Tony and Gordon don't.

I feel really bad about the day he got the news of his illness. He called me on the mobile. I was on the other phone. 'I'll call you back', I snapped, as I had done many times before. 'Ok', he said. 'It's quite important.' I didn't pick up on the tone. I called him ten minutes later. Cancer. It's odd how when he wrote about his illness he remembers me as being solid and strong and doing whatever it took to help. I felt completely pole-axed. Yet even in illness, Philip did two things he did in his political life too – he thought about others; and he sought to be strategic at all times.

These things were linked. Beating the cancer became the campaign. Once the initial shock was absorbed, and black humour could start to play its usual part in our deliberations, we developed the campaign theme: survival. There was a slogan, and a campaign song, Gloria Gaynor's finest, 'I Will Survive', occasionally mixed with the Bee Gees' 'Staying Alive' and, when he was feeling sick, the greatest of them all, the one that didn't play on Manifesto Day 2001, 'Things Can Only Get Better'. There was a grid for the hospital visits, the chemo dates, the pills, visitors, all pinned up on the kitchen fridge.

Of course, every campaign needs big vision and rhetoric and historical resonance, which I was able to provide by telling Philip of a GP I met who survived oesophageal cancer for decades by naming his cancer Hitler, and calling himself Churchill. This appealed to Philip's new-found sense of grandeur which often falls upon people when they enter the House of Lords. He would sit in his big chair by the window and go all Churchillian. 'I will fight you on the oesophagus, I will fight you on the throat, I will fight you in the mind … Never, have so many cells been seen off by so few drops of chemotherapy.'

Now you're thinking, but where does the polling come in? Well, Philip called me shortly after being first diagnosed and said 'I have had the petscan' and I said 'What's that?', and he said, 'It is basically the exit poll.' 'Oh,' I said, 'how's it looking?' To which he said, 'The momentum is with us, but clearly it's all within the margin of error.'

Even as a cancer patient he did things differently. First private in the US then the NHS in Newcastle (where he got better treatment). And when he entered what he called 'the death zone', in one of his last strategic acts, he even turned his death into a campaign, the goals of which were to make his departure easier for his wife, Gail, and their daughters, Georgia and Grace; to help others by writing and talking about facing up to death – he was dictating for a book on this almost to the very end, to which Georgia has added a beautiful account of the final days; and to update his political memoir, *The Unfinished Revolution*, with a powerful political message to Labour's next generation, to learn the right lessons from both victory and defeat. How many people write, effectively, two books when dying of cancer?

Once we all absorbed the news he had cancer, and once he set himself the task of beating it, deep down we just thought he would. Well I did. When he was off in the States, though I knew he was seriously ill, and undergoing major surgery, it never crossed my mind that he would not be coming back. When I was visiting him in Newcastle, and he was desperately trying to make sure I got on with his doctor, Mike Griffin (not New Labour's biggest fan), I didn't leave the hospital worrying I might never see him again. And even when the end came, it did so in stages, with drama, and doubt along the way. I was watching Burnley against Leicester City, on a cold Tuesday night. Philip had been due at the Marsden for chemotherapy, but before kick-off Gail called to say they had discovered he had a lung infection, which might be pneumonia, and he would have to stay in. She sounded a little more worried than usual, but she still seemed strong. He had got through worse moments than this, and though it was not the news I wanted to hear, again I assumed the doctors would treat it, then the chemo could restart when the infection was dealt with, and all would be well. Some time through the match, my phone pinged with a text. Philip was never shy of communicating deep and meaningful thoughts in a text or an email, but this one took it to the limit. 'I am fighting on but I might not beat it this time. You have been the perfect friend and you have never ever let me down. Thanks for all your support now and always. Love to all. Take care of everyone.' The players running around the pitch became a blur. I left the stand and called him, assuming he would not be able to answer but hoping someone else would. I spoke to Gail who said the doctors were very worried, and 'it might be tonight'. I left the football and began the long journey home. I cursed myself for not having seen him since the day before. I cried long and often. I kept looking at that text message, and despairing at the seeming finality of it. I spoke to Fiona and to our children, also to Tony, Sally Morgan, Peter Hyman, Anji Hunter and one or two others, and basically accepted he was gone. As when my father died, and when my best friend in journalism, John Merritt, died after a long illness, no matter how long you have had to think about it happening, and preparing yourself psychologically, when it comes, the shock is as though they were perfectly healthy and had been knocked down by a bus.

But I went into the hospital early the next morning and there he was, sitting up in bed, smiling. Admittedly it was an intensive care bed, there were tubes coming out of various parts of his body, and his head was now inside a plastic bubble that was helping him to breathe, but he could speak, and he could laugh. 'Isn't this wonderful?' he said. 'You have spent your whole life wanting to live inside your own little bubble, and I have beaten you to it.'

'Don't ever do that to me again', I said. 'What?' 'Make me think you're dead when you're not.' We talked football with a Norwich-supporting nurse called James. We talked politics. We discussed the government's health reforms. Philip and the girls helped me set questions for a quiz I was hosting later. But when the girls went to get some drinks from the café, he told me he had only a few days left, maximum.

The day he finally died, I knew he would. Philip and I had had thousands of conversations, but we also wrote to each other a lot, mainly about strategy, also about our own projects we were involved in. We wrote each other memos of advice. We gave each other plans. Sometimes we would be discussing how to handle something then Philip would say 'I'll do you a note on that' and write it out even as we were still sitting there in the same room. One of our golden rules was that 'strategy is not strategy until it is written down'. On the Saturday morning, Gail having told me he was calm and peaceful, still conscious and breathing, and accepting he had not long to live, I sat down and wrote him a letter. I wanted to set out for him what his friendship meant to me and to the family. I emailed it to him and a couple of hours later Gail told me the girls had read it to him, they were in tears but he looked happy, and he said he wanted me to read it at his funeral.

That was on the Saturday and when I woke the following morning, and spoke first thing to Gail, I could tell that she believed he was now nearing the end. All was calm, she said. He was listening to his Gregorian chants. They were not sure, however, if he could hear, or if he was aware of their presence. Fiona and I were due to attend a dinner in Manchester celebrating Sir Alex Ferguson's 25th anniversary as Manchester United manager. I was in two minds about whether to go. Gail suggested we go, but pop in to see Philip on the way to the train station. At first, Fiona didn't want to come inside the hospital. She wanted to remember him as she had last seen him, when the three of us went to visit the plot in Highgate Cemetery where his ashes were to be interred. It had been a lovely day, cold and sunny, and though he was thin, and at times struggling for breath, he had been on great form, funny, thrilled at the way his burial plot was coming along, full of warmth and advice for the future. I said she should see him one last time, and say goodbye, so we went up to the intensive care unit. He was breathing but unconscious. Gail had been told he would not come round again. She and the girls were extraordinary at that time. They knew what was coming. They had accepted it. They were determined to make his last moments as comfortable and as beautiful as they could. They were already talking about him in the past tense. The girls described his face as they read out my letter to him, and how he had raised his hand and said 'funeral, funeral', even though he and I had agreed I *wouldn't* have to speak at the funeral. An hour later, he slipped into unconsciousness.

They left us alone with him so we could say goodbye. Fiona and I each took a hand, and said a few words. I knew it would be the last time we saw him. A few hours later, as a pipe band, the Red Hot Chilli Pipers, entertained Alex Ferguson's family and friends in Manchester, I turned to Fiona and said 'I think he's gone.' I texted Gail a very neutral 'Is all ok?' She told me he had died. She had been planning not to tell me till the dinner was over. She said it was a beautiful, blissful moment and I should not be sad. She said the girls were holding a hand each, she had her hand on his back and he heaved a final breath, the Gregorian chant came to an end, and it was though a light filled the room. Then Grace said 'I think we'd better tell someone.'

Several months have passed since he died. The tears do stop. The pain of grief does subside. But he has left a huge gap in our lives, here perhaps more personal than political. Today alone I have had three decisions to make – one quite big, one small, one very trivial – that I know I would have bounced off Philip. I think I know what he would have said, in relation to all three. But I can't be sure. I have a fair share of friends, but none that I talk to every day, and literally about everything. When a close friend goes, you feel like you've lost your bearings, lost the clear sense of direction you may have had. As to what he means now, he joins a small number of friends and family who are just there, part of the fabric of one's being, someone to talk to though physically he no longer exists, someone whose counsel to imagine, someone whose lessons in life I can seek to apply after his death. Not a day will go by I won't think of him, imagine an exchange with him, see him in his daughters or in our politics, above all wish that he was here.

He was the perfect friend and he never ever let me down.

That was what I tried to tell him in the letter I wrote on the Saturday morning before his death the next day, and which I read at his funeral nine days later. Here it is.

Dear Philip,

I hope, as do so many others, that somehow you find within you the strength to carry on. The courage you have shown since the day you were told you had cancer has been inspiring. If anyone can keep on defying the medical odds, you can.

But if this does defeat you this time, I don't want you to go without me saying what a wonderful person you are, and what an extraordinary friend you have been. Of all my friends, you are the one who touches virtually every point of my life – past, present, politics, work, leisure, sport and holidays, education, books, charity, and, more important than anything, family and friendship. I have been blessed to know you. So has Fiona. So have Rory, Calum and Grace. For so many of the happiest moments of our lives, you have been there, indeed often the cause of the happiness.

You've always been there in tough times too. You remember the Alex Ferguson quote – 'the true friend is the one who walks through the door when others are putting on their coats to leave'. You have displayed that brand of friendship so often, so consistently, and with such a force as to keep me going at the lowest of moments.

When I got your moving, lovely message on Tuesday, and was convinced you wouldn't see out the night, I felt like a limb had been wrenched from me. You know my crazy theory that we only know if we have lived a good life as we approach its end – perhaps we only know the real value of a friend when we lose him. The loss for Gail, Georgia and Grace will be enormous. But so many others were touched by you and will share that loss.

My favourite quote of our time in government came not from me or you, or any of the rest of the New Labour team. It came from the Queen in the aftermath of the September 11 attacks ten years ago. 'Grief is the price we pay for love.' You are much loved. There will be much grief. But it is a price worth paying for the joy of having known you, worked with you, laughed with you, cried with you, latterly watched you face death squarely in the eye with the same humility, conviction and concern for others which you have shown in life.

I will always remember you not for the guts in facing cancer, brave though you have been, but for the extraordinary life force you have been in the healthy times. Your enthusiasm, your passion for politics, and belief in its power to do good, your love of Labour, your dedication to the cause and the team – they all have their place in the history that we all wrote together. I loved the defiant tone of your revised Unfinished Revolution, *your clear message that whatever the critics say, we changed politics and Britain for the better. So often, so many of our people weaken. You never did. You never have. You never would. That is the product of real values, strength of character, and above all integrity of spirit.*

In a world divided between givers and takers, you are the ultimate giver. In a world where prima donnas often prosper, you are the ultimate team player. Perhaps alone among the key New Labour people, you have managed to do an amazing job without making enemies. That too is a product of your extraordinary personality, your love of people and your determination always to try to build and heal. It has been humbling to see you, even in these last days and weeks, trying to heal some of the wounds that came with the pressures of power. We can all take lessons from that, and we all should.

Of course I will miss the daily chats, the banter, the unsettled argument about whether QPR are a bigger club than Burnley. More, I'll miss your always being on hand to help me think something through, large or small. But what I will miss more than anything is the life force, the big voice. You have made our lives so much better. You are part of our lives and you will be forever. Because in my life, Philip, you are a bigger force than the death that is about to take you.

The Start of Labour's Long March: 1985–1992

3

Patricia Hewitt

It is impossible to understand the scale of Philip Gould's contribution to Labour politics without remembering just how bad things were for Labour after the 1983 defeat. For most British voters – the people whom Labour claimed to represent – Labour was, quite simply, 'beyond the pale'.

That was the stark heading of the research presentation in November 1985 that Philip later described as 'the most important of any presented during the entire period I worked with the Labour Party'. The all-day Saturday session brought together the core of what would become, a few months later, Labour's Shadow Communications Agency (SCA): Leslie Butterfield and Paul Southgate from the advertising agency Abbott Mead Vickers, Roddy Glen from the Strategic Research Group Ltd, Chris Powell from BMP and Deborah Mattinson from Ayer Barker, who became Philip's business partner the following year and later established her own business, Opinion Leader Research. Robin Cook was there as Neil Kinnock's campaign coordinator in the Shadow Cabinet; Peter Mandelson had started as Labour's director of communications a month earlier; I represented Neil's office, having been his press secretary since his election as leader in autumn 1983.

After hours listening to a key group of voters – women aged 25–44 – Leslie, Paul and Roddy summarised their findings in a simple table, a rectangle divided into three blocks. The largest, in the middle, was the acceptable centre ground of politics, where reasonable people could disagree. Flanking it on either side were 'Left Wing Beyond the Pale' and 'Right Wing Beyond the Pale'. For these voters, who would be critical to any future Labour victory, the centre block was almost entirely full of Conservative policies. The 'right-wing' block was almost empty. But most Labour policies – unilateral nuclear disarmament, repealing Tory trade union legislation, renationalizing utilities – were 'left-wing beyond the pale'.

To make matters worse, as Philip recounts in *The Unfinished Revolution*,[1] these voters were voluble in describing Labour's madness: as Roddy Glen remembered, they talked about socialism, communism, extremism, reds, and the loony left. But they had no equivalent language for the extreme right: indeed, it scarcely figured on their radar, so successful had Margaret Thatcher been in reframing her brand of brutal neo-liberalism as down-to-earth common sense.

None of this came as a surprise to Philip. The child of two teachers, he had an ordinary upbringing, not deprived but suburban. Although always instinctively Labour, he didn't imbibe any of the Labour Party's tribal truths from his parents (he described his father's politics as 'non-conformist, individualist, Liberal', those of his Dutch mother as continental socialist). Condemned to an appalling secondary modern after failing the 11-plus, he always had an instinctive sympathy for working-class attitudes and aspirations. By the 1983 general election, sitting miserably alone in his small London flat, he knew that 'Labour had not merely stopped listening or lost touch: it had declared political war on the values, instincts and ethics of the great majority of decent, hard-working voters'.[2]

That same night, I was equally miserably watching the count in Leicester East, a supposedly safe Labour seat that I was fighting against the sitting MP, Tom Bradley, a defector to the Social Democrats. In an agonisingly close three-way campaign, Labour lost to the Conservatives. After five recounts, we also lost Leicester South and only just hung on to Leicester West (where Greville Janner and his father before him had represented the constituency since 1945 and where I would be elected in 1997). Nationally, Labour's vote slumped below 28 per cent, the lowest level since 1918.

I did not meet Philip until two years later. And my route into Labour politics could hardly have been more different. A fourth-generation Australian, I was born in Canberra where I absorbed a commitment to public service from my parents (my father a senior public servant, my mother a university lecturer), but learnt nothing of party politics. Both my parents had suffered from the loss of their father at an early age; as a young man, my father had bitter experience of the depression in 1930s Melbourne. But my own childhood was comfortable and, in many ways, privileged. Coming to the UK in the late 1960s to study at Cambridge, I was inspired by student politics and feminism, campaigned for women's rights, went to work for Age Concern and then Liberty (in those days the National Council for Civil Liberties), joined the Labour Party and the TGWU and made long-lasting friendships, amongst them with Harriet Harman, Margaret Hodge and Charles Clarke. I have never lost my feminism or commitment to social justice. But it was the 1983 general election campaign – meeting one voter after another, listed on our canvass records as solid Labour, who laughed or slammed the door in my face – that taught me the folly of the election manifesto I had so enthusiastically supported. The lessons that Philip learned in Woking as a child, I learned in Leicester in 1983.

Labour had to change. And the change started with the election of Neil Kinnock as leader at the 1983 party conference. I scarcely knew him – I'd met him with mutual friends a year or so earlier, he'd spoken brilliantly at a rally in Leicester during the campaign and, with thousands of others, I had been moved to tears by his devastating eve-of-poll speech: 'If Margaret Thatcher wins on Thursday, I warn you not to be ordinary, I warn you not to be young, I warn you not to fall ill, I warn you not to get old.' Kinnock knew Labour had to change its policies, using the leadership election itself to signal an abandonment of Labour's pledge to withdraw from the Common Market. He knew Labour had to change, completely, its approach to campaigns and communications after the unspeakable shambles of the 1983 campaign. (The slogan 'Think positive, act positive, vote Labour' was bad enough. When I sat down to watch the party election broadcasts – dull, dark, miserable – I was grateful I hadn't had the time to watch them during the campaign itself.) When Neil asked me to become his press secretary, I accepted enthusiastically, joining Charles Clarke, former *Tribune* editor Dick Clements, John Newbigin, Sue Nye (later the lynchpin of Gordon Brown's office), and, later, Jan Royall and John Eatwell. But all too soon, we were engulfed in the miners' strike, with voters repelled by the NUM's failure to ballot as well as by outbreaks of violence on the picket line, and Neil himself caught between his knowledge that the strike was doomed, his fury with Arthur Scargill's posturing and his own deep roots in the Welsh mining valleys.

Any attempt at serious modernization had to wait until after the end of the strike. Larry Whitty, the new general secretary, restructured the party's headquarters at Walworth Road, creating a new directorate of campaigns and communications. Neil persuaded a narrow majority of the NEC to appoint Peter Mandelson, then at London Weekend Television, to the new post. Arriving in October 1985, Peter immediately commissioned Philip to carry out a complete review of Labour's communications and campaigning. It was the start of an extraordinary alliance that would revolutionise British political campaigning.

But before then, Neil Kinnock had himself taken the first, dramatic step in Labour's long march to electability with his party conference attack on the Militant Liverpool City Council leader, Derek Hatton. Militant had long pursued a Trotskyite strategy of 'entryism' into the Labour Party, colonising local branches, intimidating other members and exercising an increasingly malign influence on Labour policy. At Bournemouth, in September 1985, Kinnock struck: 'I'll tell you what happens with impossible promises. You start with far-fetched resolutions. They are then pickled into a rigid dogma, a code, and you go through the years sticking to that – outdated, misplaced, irrelevant to real needs. You end in the grotesque chaos of a Labour council – a *Labour* council – hiring taxis to scuttle round a city handing out redundancy notices to its own workers.' By now, there was uproar in the conference hall. Hatton was on his feet, shouting, arms waving, walking out. For a heart-stopping moment, it seemed as if the conference would collapse in chaos. But Neil's courage and sheer fury won out: 'I'm telling you, you can't play politics with people's jobs and with people's lives.' It was the defining moment of Neil's leadership.

An embryonic Shadow Communications Agency already existed, the 'Breakfast Group' of communications experts convened by Chris Powell on behalf of Robin Cook. It included Philip and Deborah Mattinson, as well as Roddy Glen and Leslie Butterfield who tested voter reactions in focus groups before and after Neil's speech. The reactions were extraordinary. Neil had cut through voters' indifference, seizing their attention by placing himself on the side of the public against the extremists in his own party – a strategy that he, and later Tony Blair, would repeat to good effect in the years to come. But the speech was just the beginning of months of desperately hard work as Neil and Charles prepared and prosecuted the case against Militant that would, finally, lead to an NEC decision to expel its leaders and change the party's rules. Quite simply, there was no one else to do it. It was energy-sapping, soul-destroying stuff – but it finally removed one of the reasons why Labour was beyond the pale.

The Bournemouth speech drove a wedge between the 'hard' and the 'soft' left of the Labour Party, creating a new Kinnockite majority on the NEC and starting to open up space for modernisation. Not all Kinnock's supporters were happy, but they were forced to choose. Into this highly-charged atmosphere came Peter Mandelson and Philip Gould.

Looking back, I can't remember my first meeting with Philip. I simply remember him being always there. In and out of the Leader's Office at the end of a dark House of Commons corridor under Big Ben. Shaggy-haired, rumpled, scattering papers and ideas with wonderful energy and creativity, he became the person none of us could do without. Politics is a world full of large and often fragile egos (generally male) competing for attention. Philip was different. He didn't want the limelight. He was warmly interested in other people, taking the trouble to turn colleagues into friends, generous with his time, hospitality and praise. But without arrogance, he also had an extraordinary sense of the contribution he could make to his beloved Labour Party. Despite the trauma of his secondary schooling, he'd got himself to university, to a Master's in politics, to the London Business School as a Sloan Fellow. He'd not only learnt about business and advertising – at a time when Labour despised both – he'd set up and then sold his own advertising business, buying a house in Notting Hill that Gail made beautifully welcoming. Gail was herself extraordinary, using a redundancy payment from her first job to establish a small publishing house that proved so successful it engineered a reverse takeover of a much larger firm. I was in awe of her. But most astonishing, at least to me, Philip had set himself up as a political consultant – in those days, a creature most of us had never heard of. He was actively defining himself, creating his role in life, in a way that I'd hardly come across before. I wouldn't have put it like this at the time, but what I was seeing was Philip's determination to be the author of his own life.

Once Peter and Philip were on board, things moved fast. Philip's 64-page report to Peter on Labour communications became the blueprint for change. Chris Powell had already begun to assemble a shadow advertising and market research team – 'shadow' because no reputable agency would risk taking Labour as a client. Philip became its coordinator, convening twelve sub-groups including a writers' group chaired by Ken Follett and involving Hanif Kureishi, Colin Welland and Melvyn Bragg and initiating 17 different projects, from general election and leader's campaign planning to targeting, direct mail and corporate image. Bob Worcester, head of MORI, continued to handle opinion polls, as he had done for many years, but with Philip often drafting the questions and writing the analysis. Focus groups became increasingly influential (and, in 1992, were to prove considerably more accurate than the polls themselves.) Ratified by the NEC several months later – but still the object of deep suspicion amongst many Labour MPs and

NEC members – the Shadow Communications Agency became a fact of Labour life.

The Agency's first election campaign was the Fulham by-election on 10 April 1986, a Conservative seat that all the pundits expected the SDP to win. But while both Conservative and SDP candidates lived outside the constituency, Nick Raynsford was a highly effective local councillor. Deborah Mattinson persuaded one of her advertising colleagues, Trevor Beattie, to devise our campaign. Trevor bypassed all the usual turgid Labour campaign material and produced the eye-catching line 'Nick Raynsford Lives Here', complete with cheeky leaflet featuring an A to Z page of Fulham and suggesting that while Nick had been busy building new landmarks for local people, the other candidates were struggling to find the constituency. We won the seat with a swing of over 10 per cent.

Meanwhile, Philip and Peter were busy with the SCA's social policy group, developing the 'Freedom and Fairness' campaign for Kinnock and the NEC. 'Fairness' was a traditional Labour value, but Neil was also determined to reclaim 'freedom' from the Tories. We wanted 'symbolic policies' that would appeal to voters and Neil welcomed the inclusion of issues such as a greater say for NHS patients alongside more traditional Labour offers such as higher child benefit. But he hadn't expected Labour's old yellow and red stickers to be replaced by a new, edgy, black, silver and grey. Nor was he happy when 'freedom and fairness' disappeared in favour of 'Putting People First', although Peter brokered a last-minute compromise with 'Labour's Freedom and Fairness Campaign' added in small print to all the leaflets and posters. But he loved the campaign launch, at the International Press Centre near Fleet Street instead of the usual scruffy Labour rooms; he was fluent and at ease with the new positioning; and he enchanted the photographers by hugging the small girl featured in the campaign material and swinging her into the air. Eric Heffer, who had stormed out after the Bournemouth speech, scowled from the back of the room, complaining that this wasn't the Labour Party he'd joined. Political journalists and commentators felt the same way, with *The Economist* and the *Financial Times* as well as the *Guardian* and *Tribune* hailing it as a breath of fresh air for Labour.

The next stage from Philip's initial stock-take was the blandly titled 'review of corporate appearance'. If the NEC had realised the intention was to abandon Labour's old macho symbols – the red flag and clenched fist – they wouldn't have nodded it through. But Neil wanted the change and, inspired by Labour's sister Scandinavian parties, himself proposed a red rose. Philip and Peter brought in one of Britain's top designers, Michael Wolff, who commissioned the artist Philip Sutton. In July, Philip, Peter, Michael and I went to Sutton's south London home, where every inch of wall, every piece of furniture sang with vibrant colour. In his studio, dozens of images of roses were pegged to a washing line for us to pore over. After an intense few hours, we agreed a shortlist. There were still worries, however: yes, the rose was new, different, fresh and optimistic. But was it too wishy-washy, too feminine? Michael Wolff persevered, working with Sutton to produce an image that we all loved. Launched at the 1986 party conference, the rose was a triumph.

By then, Philip had already started on general election campaign planning. I was on maternity leave for the second half of 1986 and Philip would come to see me at home, joining me at the kitchen table where I cradled my baby daughter on my lap, as we painstakingly translated campaign ideas into a week-by-week, day-by-day and then hour-by-hour grid. No campaign software in those days; we worked with pencil, ruler and rubber, three weeks reduced to a page, discarded papers piling up as they became illegible. But we had one crucial insight: that this would be Britain's first real television campaign. As Philip recalled:

We wanted to focus on television; ensure brilliant, memorable pictures; provide stories that fed into every stage of the news cycle; concentrate on the leader and a small group of key campaigners; plan the campaign around the discipline of a tightly controlled daily grid. This is how the 1987

election was fought and it is essentially how Labour has fought every
national election since.[3]

Every day was allocated a theme, reflecting our strengths in
education, jobs and, above all, health. Every day, not only the press
conference and leaflets but, vitally, every campaign visit and photo
opportunity would reflect that theme. It was a simple enough
device, but it hadn't been used before. It gave us an extraordinary
degree of control over the television images, to the point where the
media became increasingly frustrated as the campaign developed.
But it meant that, even when the entire media scrum was chasing
Neil on defence policy – one of our critical weaknesses – all the
pictures showed Neil in hospitals, listening to nurses and patients.

Our campaign planning, however, was thrown off course by
the Greenwich by-election in January 1987, where Labour's
candidate, a hard-left former London councillor, Deirdre Wood,
lost decisively to the SDP. Matters were made worse by Neil's visit
to Washington in March, when his brief meeting with President
Reagan – who mistook Denis Healey for the British Ambassador
and mumbled his way through a largely inaudible script – was
turned by the White House spinners and the British media into a
massive snub to Kinnock and Labour's defence policy.

The truth was, despite the expulsion of Militant and our brilliant
new communications strategy, Labour had not really changed.
Philip, clear-sighted as ever, warned about our vulnerability, not
only on defence and tax, but fundamentally on trust. He knew
from the focus groups that voters felt despairing at the thought of
another Conservative victory. It was an election the Conservatives
should have lost. But as he said at the time, people did not trust
Labour. The only hope was an emotional campaign, based on
social issues, hitting the Tories as hard as we could and balancing
the negative campaign with Kinnock's positive appeal.

A week before the election was called, opinion polls confirmed
Philip's gloomy assessment. Labour and the Liberal-SDP Alliance
were neck and neck, splitting the anti-Tory vote. One even
put Labour in third place. Far from an election where Labour

challenged the Tories for victory, it looked as if the only story of the campaign would be whether Labour was pushed into third place. The 1987 campaign – Philip's first as a political strategist – saved the Labour Party from a defeat from which it would never have recovered.

The tide began to turn with Neil's extraordinary speech at Llandudno: 'Why am I the first Kinnock in a thousand generations to go to university?' Filming it was Hugh Hudson, the genius of *Chariots of Fire*, whom Peter and I had commissioned to produce a party election broadcast about Neil. Reflecting Philip's strategy, I wrote a brief designed to counteract each of Neil's vulnerabilities, making him the positive heart of our campaign. Alastair Campbell – then political editor of the *Daily Mirror* and Neil's staunchest press supporter – interviewed friends and colleagues, including Barbara Castle, who countered suspicions of Kinnock's weakness: 'There's steel at the heart of that young man.' Hugh and his team worked magic. They'd spent a precious day with Neil and Glenys on the coast of south Wales, filming the opening sequence – swooping down from a fighter jet to a seagull above the cliffs – and the closing images of Neil and Glenys hand in hand. The interviews, the assault on Militant at Bournemouth, the Llandudno speech, all came together in a portrait of a visionary, inspiring leader whose values were matched by his toughness. Philip and I spent hours with Hugh and his film editor in a tiny Soho studio, going back and forth over every cut and join (this was before the glorious days of digital editing). But it was Peter who added the audacious final touch, ending the broadcast not with the usual campaign slogan and Labour logo, but with the one word, Kinnock. Neil's ratings rose overnight by 16 points.

'Chariots of Kinnock' became the symbol of a brilliant campaign that sealed both Peter's and Philip's reputations. A brilliant campaign, but another massive defeat. For all the campaigning, for all the agony of expelling Militant, for all the power of Neil's words, we had only crawled from the 27.6 per cent of 1983 to 31 per cent of the vote. For millions of people who had previously voted Labour or whose parents had always voted Labour, we were still beyond the pale. But it was enough – enough to defeat the Alliance, enough to give Labour another chance.

In many ways, 1987 was the high point of Neil's leadership, the height especially of his extraordinary rhetorical power. As Tony Blair was to say after 1994, it was Neil who created the foundations upon which New Labour was built.

But far more fundamental change was needed. After the election, Tom Sawyer, one of Neil's staunchest supporters on the NEC and subsequently a general secretary of the party, told Neil Labour needed a radical review of its policy. Policy Review groups were set up, co-chaired by members of the Shadow Cabinet and the NEC, to look at every aspect of economic, social, defence and foreign policy. Roy Hattersley prepared a statement of Labour values to provide a philosophical underpinning to the review and reassure party members that, far from abandoning Labour's traditional values, we were in fact applying them to the modern world.

Neil asked Philip, Peter and myself to set the tone for the Policy Review by analysing the new world to which Labour had to adjust. We brought in new recruits – Roger Jowell of the British Social Attitudes surveys; Paul Ormerod from the Henley Centre for Forecasting; Andrew McIntosh of the market research company IFF – to supplement the SCA team. The final result – 'Britain and Labour in the 1990s' – was a far-reaching analysis of demographic, social and economic change, charting the decline in Labour's vote over 20 years (while Tory support had remained solid), the shift from manufacturing to services and unionised to non-unionised workplaces, the feminisation of the labour market, the rise of individualism and the impact of technology and globalisation.

It wasn't comfortable reading for Labour traditionalists. Philip undertook the 'terrifying ordeal' of presenting the findings to the NEC and Shadow Cabinet in November 1987. As he recalls: 'At the end of the presentation there was silence ... Most people in the room applauded. The SCA had let off a bomb in the heart of Labour.' Philip remained a key figure throughout the Policy Review, marshalling groups of researchers to support each of the review groups.

Neil intended 'Britain and Labour in the 1990s' to give the Policy Review groups the impetus – and, if necessary, the excuse – for fresh thinking and new ideas. I returned from maternity leave after the birth of my second baby in early 1988, to a new role as policy coordinator, charged by Neil with getting as much as we could out of the Policy Review. I spent hours drafting, redrafting, chivvying and brainstorming in the search for attractive new ideas. At Neil's request, I largely rewrote the draft on welfare reform, with which Neil was particularly unhappy, but to little avail.

With the exception of the defence group, where Gerald Kaufman skilfully abandoned unilateralism, the Policy Review generated little in the way of radical thinking. Most of the energy went into arguments about how far to move from the old, rather than how to create the new. On the utilities, for instance, the economic review groups eventually agreed that we should no longer pledge wholesale renationalisation – by then, a completely lost cause with voters – but failed to do the thinking that was really needed about effective regulation, how to promote competition or how to encourage new forms of ownership by employees and consumers. In the words of a Democratic Congressman that I quoted at the time: 'We have scrubbed off the graffiti of the past, but we have not yet painted the mural of the future.'

Philip knew that, if Labour was ever going to win, we not only needed to increase our support generally but we also had to close the gender gap in British politics – the markedly higher support for the Conservatives amongst women, who were even more likely than men to be turned off by Labour. Deborah Mattinson and I believed we needed to listen to women voters far more closely, organising a series of focus groups where we heard women talk about politics almost entirely through the eyes of their family. Even young women who hadn't yet had children anticipated their family's needs in all their responses, while older women strongly identified with the needs of their grown-up children and grandchildren. As Deborah described it:

> Despite protesting that politics was not for them, women were very much
> more likely than men to be involved in 'quasi political activity': parent-teacher
> associations, housing and tenants' organisations. They were experts. Yet
> they tended to discount this experience, not regarding it as 'proper politics'.
> Politics, they believed, were the abstract matters discussed by their male
> partners in pubs and trade union meetings. Politics wasn't for them.[4]

The result was that, even though they preferred Labour policies
and shared Labour's 'caring' values and although Labour had more
women MPs than any other party, they felt profoundly alienated
from Labour. We presented the results to the Shadow Cabinet
(and later published them in a Fabian Society pamphlet, *Women's
Votes: The Key to Winning*). The only other woman there was
Jo Richardson, the shadow women's minister, and many of her
male colleagues shuffled their papers as we spoke. But we got
somewhere with our simple argument that they would only become
government ministers with women's support. Crucially, we already
had Neil's backing. The result was a new target for increasing the
number of Labour women candidates and the addition of three
Shadow Cabinet places, reserved for women. We also continued
to insist on the inclusion of women in election broadcasts and
press conference platforms, and introduced the highly successful
women's magazine lookalike, highlighting Labour policies through
human interest stories. Philip was much less interested in all this,
believing that if we could get wholesale transformation of Labour's
policies and positioning, women voters would follow.

Alongside the Policy Review, Philip was concentrating on the
European Parliament elections to be held in June 1989. Our
position at the start of the year was dire. We were eleven points
behind in the polls; morale amongst Labour supporters was low
and we were making no progress on extremism, high taxes, nationalisation and opposition to council house sales, all the issues that
were vital to voters' trust. All the predictions were that Labour
would lose seats: gains seemed unimaginable. Philip completely
turned that round. At the critical meeting of the campaign team
in February that year, he told us that if Labour was to have any

chance at the general election in 1992, we had to win the European elections in 1989 – and win them decisively. As he presented his analysis, the response was incredulous. As he said, 'everyone fell about laughing'. But his logic was unassailable, his energy and enthusiasm irresistible. By the end of the meeting, everyone was signed up. We were going to win new seats – and the only way of doing that was to bring the Policy Review forward to create momentum and persuade people that Labour had changed.

It was in this campaign note – and Philip's notes became a famous part of his style as a political consultant – that Philip first talked about 'New Labour'. (I had used the phrase earlier, trying to persuade Neil to highlight it in a speech.) 'New Labour has lost its zest and modernity', Philip wrote. He wanted to use the European campaign and the Policy Review to persuade the public that 'Labour has changed. Neil Kinnock has delivered a New Labour party.'[5] The original plan had been to delay the launch of the Policy Review and trickle it out as a series of separate documents, designed to minimise backlash from within the party. Philip changed all that, demanding – and getting – a big bang.

Philip suggests in his book that Neil didn't put enough effort into steering the Policy Review where he wanted it to go. In fact, Neil was himself wrestling with how far Labour should change – for instance, from being a party of the producer to a party for the consumer. I remember an away-day he led with his own office, early in the Policy Review, where he was still arguing, as he'd long believed, 'you can't control what you don't own'. He believed he'd given his colleagues a clear enough steer about what was needed – but he also worried about how far and how fast he could push the party to change. But as the drafts began to come through, he shared the unhappiness that Philip, Peter, Charles Clarke and I all felt.

Instead, as the European elections approached, we had to make the best of what we had, highlighting in particular the new defence policy. Between us, we managed to get enough – or just enough – modernising content agreed in the rest of the review, to be highlighted in large, bold print in the final documents. (Most of them were so long that we knew few people would read the detail.) Barry Delaney, a leading advertising figure, came up with the title: 'Meet the Challenge, Make the Change', designed to suggest that what we were doing for the party, we would also do for Britain. In truth, the Policy Review promised far more than it delivered. But it was enough to give us the impetus that we needed. And combined with Tory divisions and their disastrous 'diet of Brussels' campaign, it gave us victory in the European elections.

Neil himself had already come to the conclusion that what Labour really needed was an independent think-tank to do the kind of radical thinking for the left that established think tanks had done for conservatives in both the United States and Britain. That was the inspiration for the Institute for Public Policy Research (IPPR), which opened its doors in early 1989, with James Cornford as its first director and myself as his deputy. I hadn't found it easy returning after maternity leave and Philip was extraordinarily kind and wise in his advice. But the decision to move on turned out to be absolutely right; I loved the freedom we had and the chance to help create what became new Labour's most influential and successful think tank.

The European victory was not the springboard for 1992 that Philip intended. The truth was that, despite the brilliant presentation of the Policy Review, far too little had really changed. To compound the problem, we no longer had the 1987 campaign structure and team. Peter had decided, rightly and with Philip's and my blessing, to stand for Parliament and was selected for Hartlepool at the end of 1989. Sadly, with Neil and Charles both angered by what they saw as a betrayal, Peter left Walworth Road in October 1990. Although I continued to work on the Policy Review and the 1992 election campaign, I was doing so from the outside. As the general election approached, the campaign structure became increasingly chaotic. Philip struggled on, desperately trying to hold the show together. He created a weekly Campaign Advisory Team (CAT), chaired by Jack Cunningham, the campaign coordinator, although he couldn't get Peter accepted as a member. The meeting at least brought the key people together. But it suffered from a fatal flaw – it was designed to be secret. So Philip would rush from the unofficial secret meeting to the official one at Walworth Road, large, unwieldy and not surprisingly suspicious of decisions that seemed to be coming from nowhere. Separately, Philip was chairing meetings of the SCA, which became increasingly influential – and, as a result, the target of growing hostility. As the official campaign structures disintegrated, Philip and I were asked to take on more and more responsibility. In December 1991, Philip delivered the 'War Book', his complete plan for the election campaign, predicting with frightening accuracy the Conservative attacks on tax, Kinnock himself, trade unions and extremism. By Christmas, the campaign was in crisis. Once again, Philip and I sat down to plan a campaign grid, this time taking us from January 1992 until the likely election in April or May. But a week into January, the Conservatives hit us with their 'Tax Bombshell' campaign and a few months later launched their election campaign with the slogan 'You Can't Trust Labour'. As Philip sadly recalled: 'By the start of the election a campaign machine that had been brilliant in 1987 and strong in 1990 had weakened almost to breaking-point.'

In this dreadful atmosphere of paranoia and suspicion, with relationships fractured, Peter banished, the election campaign team itself splintered between Walworth Road, Millbank and the SCA headquarters at Transport House and Neil increasingly criticised by his own colleagues and doubting his own leadership, Philip performed heroically. He was the rock, the lynchpin of the campaign. But nothing that he or the rest of us did could change the fundamentals. The autumn before the election, I prepared a paper for the CAT, spelling out that 'fear of taxes is the single most important reason for not voting Labour'. Charles was furious; terrified of destabilising the fragile truce between Neil and John Smith, he insisted that all copies be destroyed. In the Policy Review, undeterred by all the SCA's opinion research, Smith had committed Labour to increases in child benefit and pensions that by 1992 simply couldn't be afforded. The last straw was the Conservatives' budget just before the campaign started, when Norman Lamont announced the introduction of a 20p tax band. We were trapped, unable to abandon the promised benefit increases, equally unable to withdraw a tax band designed to help lower-income workers and, worst of all, committed to scrapping the upper limit on national insurance contributions – a massive tax hike for those just above average pay. We made the best of it all at Labour's shadow budget, held in the oak-panelled hall of the Institute of Civil Engineers in Westminster, crammed with journalists, analysts and business-people. Designed to make Labour look like a party of government, the shadow budget gave us a day's favourable television news – and three weeks' relentless media attacks.

The plan was to switch from our weakest territory to our strongest – health – with a hard-hitting election broadcast. But 'Jennifer's Ear' – a compelling account of the different fortunes of two little girls – one treated privately, the other by the NHS – collapsed in disarray when details of the family whose case had inspired the broadcast were given to the press. (Ironically, Philip had actually commissioned a far more hard-hitting health broadcast that was never used.) Behind the media drama was a complete breakdown of communications between Philip (who had consistently opposed any link with real cases), the shadow health team and Labour press officers. Eight days before the poll, the Sheffield rally that Philip and I had planned as a turbo-charge for the last week proved a damp squib, not even making it to the top of the TV news.

In the middle of all this, Philip's father was taken seriously ill. He went straight down to Weybridge, where he found his father dying of cancer. For the rest of the campaign, he visited daily and was with his father when he died.

Despite tax, despite Jennifer's Ear, despite all the internal chaos, by the Tuesday evening before election day, the opinion polls were putting Labour ahead. As usual, we had advance warning of some of the polls that the press would publish the next day. Over a rushed supper, we agreed that our own private poll was probably more accurate. But even that put us several points ahead. We dared to think that the result might in fact be a hung Parliament, with Labour the largest party. (It was many months before we all learned that, in fact, a whole series of sampling errors had added up to a substantial polling bias against the Tories.)

The evening before the election, as Philip and I walked back from Millbank to the SCA headquarters just off Smith Square, we saw John Major standing near the Tory campaign bus with a small group of supporters. In his account, Philip describes him as 'forlorn and lonely'. My own recollection is different; as Major recognised us and we turned away, I have always remembered Philip saying 'That doesn't look like a man who knows he's going to lose.' Philip was, rightly, convinced that, although the public did not want to vote Tory, we had failed to persuade them to turn to Labour. Although the early exit polls still suggested a hung Parliament, by a few hours later the scale of Major's triumph was all too clear. As dawn broke, Neil Kinnock – whose brave leadership had laid the foundations for New Labour's landslide five years later – announced his resignation as party leader.

The attack on the campaign, the Shadow Communications Agency and, above all, Philip and myself began immediately. Many of those who had praised the campaign, worked alongside us, endorsed the strategy and predicted success, were quick to vilify 'metropolitan, middle-class' peddlers of 'glitz and gloss'. I at least could return to the friendship and sanity of the IPPR (where John Smith almost immediately asked me to organise the Commission on Social Justice, designed to review Labour's tax and benefits policies – or, to put it more bluntly, get us off the hook of the shadow budget. I became the Commission's deputy chair; its secretary was David Miliband; and its work made an important contribution to New Labour's policy agenda). But Philip, demonstrating quite extraordinary resilience, commissioned immediate telephone polling to find out what had really happened. The results were devastating. As Philip had warned, Labour had failed to lay to rest the deep-seated fears of our extremism, our economic incompetence and, above all, Labour's apparent hostility to voters' ambitions for a better life. At a grim post mortem meeting of the SCA, Philip described the extraordinary, almost atavistic, terror that voters felt. As one woman had told the pollsters on Friday night, in the first wave of post-election polling: 'I was going to vote Labour. I went into the polling booth intending to vote Labour. But I couldn't bring myself to make that cross. I just thought if Labour wins, something terrible is going to happen.' The notorious *Sun* headline – 'IF KINNOCK WINS TODAY WILL THE LAST PERSON IN BRITAIN PLEASE TURN OUT THE LIGHTS' – had not created, but had brilliantly summed up swing voters' deepest fears. It was not a message Labour wanted to hear.

The 1992 campaign tested Philip to the limits. The strain was appalling, the attacks on him grossly unfair, leaving him drained and depressed. But in these seven years and, perhaps most of all in this second campaign, he had discovered the extent of his personal strength, forging close relationships with Neil Kinnock, Gordon Brown, Tony Blair and Peter Mandelson, keeping communication open even with his critics, learning to use his charm and energy to inspire and mobilise a team. He had carved out the new role for himself that he had begun to dream of as a teenager in Woking, becoming Labour's first modern political strategist and revolutionising political campaigning in Britain. Above all, his instinctive belief that Labour had to return to suburban swing voters before they would return Labour to government had been reinforced by two more election defeats, poll upon poll, focus group after focus group, leading him to the unshakeable conviction that Labour had to become New Labour. The Long March to electability still had a long way to go – and Philip himself still had much to do.

Notes

1. Philip Gould, *The Unfinished Revolution: How the Modernisers Saved the Labour Party* (Little, Brown, 1998), pp. 51ff. All references are to the 1998 edition unless otherwise specified.
2. Gould, *Unfinished Revolution*, p. 19.
3. Gould, *Unfinished Revolution*, p. 67.

4. Deborah Mattinson, *Talking to a Brick Wall: How New Labour Stopped Listening to the Voter and Why We Need a New Politics* (Biteback, 2010), p. 45.
5. Gould, *Unfinished Revolution*, pp. 96–97.

The Unstarted Revolution

4

Peter Mandelson

The New Labour revolution spanned 25 years of Philip Gould's life, from 1985 to the party's election defeat in 2010. It was a rollercoaster ride for him, while consuming the energies and passions of a generation of activists, as the party – eventually - chalked up three major election victories in a row.

These wins were undoubtedly exciting, but the early period of Philip's endeavours, up to 1992, reveals the tough, painstaking origin of these victories and what was done in those difficult years to lay the foundation for them.

Being in Opposition is a very frustrating time when you are expected to lay siege to everything the government is doing while trying to rebuild your own credibility and belief in your own future policies as you do so. All of us involved in the pre-New Labour period in the 1980s felt that we were doing not just what an ordinary Opposition has to do but more, much more: that we were fighting for our party's very existence, with an alternative to Labour in the field in the form of the newly formed Social Democratic Party. We experienced a huge wave of relief and anticipation when by 1989 we believed that, at last, we were firmly back on track. But it proved to be a false dawn, raising then dashing our hopes, as we awaited further defeat in 1992 before going on to win our landslide in 1997.

The Adman Cometh

There is no doubt what brought Philip Gould into the service of the Labour Party: to help rescue it from oblivion and turn it, once more, into an electorally successful and progressive force of government. After 13 years of being just that, for many it is hard, if not impossible, now to imagine what we went through to get there. The direct political involvement of Labour's current generation began not at the time of Labour's near-death experience in the 1980s, but the 1990s when we were well on our way back to power.

Philip's own words in his book *The Unfinished Revolution: How the Modernisers Saved the Labour Party* sum up the state of the party in those days: 'completely demoralized and riven from top to bottom by rivalry, hatred and dissent'.

Our wretched state did not stem from what others were doing to us but what we did to ourselves. It is not that Labour lost the will to win but that, by drifting further and further out of touch with mainstream voters, we mistook what we needed to do in order to win. We persuaded ourselves that our policies, totally out of touch with the times, were what these voters wanted to vote for; in doing so we entered a sort of parallel political universe.

We were not sleepwalking to defeat; internal arguments were so fierce that rest let alone sleep was impossible. We were wide awake. Labour had become the angry party, directing anger at the Tories and their public spending and job cuts, at the media for not fully endorsing our attacks and at our own leaders for not offering a pure enough alternative. Our activists believed that Mrs Thatcher was an ideological extremist and that this gave us permission to offer our own equivalent on the left. There was little understanding that the Thatcher brand – with its rejection of high taxes, militant unions, 'wasteful' public spending and state ownership of utilities and industry – went with the grain of public opinion, whereas few voters thought Labour's brand and its policy prescriptions worked any more. It was clear from all available polling that, in fact, the public would have preferred a more centrist position, one that was more moderate but modern and accepting of the realities of life and what needed to be done. They did not think Labour offered a centrist alternative to Mrs Thatcher's doctrinaire approach. For Labour, insofar as there was discussion of the electoral centre ground, it was assumed that the Tories' policies, as well as disappointment with the previous Labour government's 'betrayal' of the party's principles, had moved voters to the left. But there was no evidence for this.

The 1983 general election has entered party folklore, for good reason. The most vote-losing policies were articulated by the most unelectable Labour leader presiding over the most chaotic campaign, ever. But this was no simple headquarters' defeat. It flowed from the condition of the party and what most of its activists demanded. This had already resulted in the departure of a swathe of party members and MPs, led by Roy Jenkins, Shirley Williams, David Owen and Bill Rodgers, the so-called Gang of Four, to form the SDP. In the wake of the terrible 1983 election defeat, the party cemented its leftward tilt by opting for the Tribunite Neil Kinnock as its next leader over the centrist former Cabinet minister, Roy Hattersley. The message from Kinnock's supporters was 'we want to be elected but we don't want to compromise too much with the voters to get there'.

This captured Kinnock's soft left outlook – we need to change for sure but our fundamental thinking must remain the same. However, he did not offer his party a quiet life. He was determined to turn round Labour's fortunes which he believed were being destroyed by the party's hard left. After fumbling (to his subsequent regret) the year-long miners' strike in 1984–85, Kinnock launched a crusade to create a new model party, free of the Trotskyists and their malign influence and of the Bennites' tolerance of their entryism.

It was an inspiring and brave fight-back, beginning with the most dramatic and powerful conference speech ever delivered by a Labour leader. To roars of applause from constituency and trade union delegates alike, Kinnock, in 1985, took aim at the Militant leadership of Liverpool City Council:

> Implausible promises don't win victories. I'll tell you what happens with impossible promises. You start with far-fetched resolutions. They are then pickled into a rigid dogma, a code, and you go through the years sticking to that, outdated, misplaced, irrelevant to the real needs, and you end in the grotesque chaos of a Labour council – a *Labour* council – hiring taxis to

scuttle round a city handing out redundancy notices to its own workers ...
You can't play politics with people's jobs.

The battle for the soul of the Labour Party was, at last, engaged.
After a year of legal and publicity battles, in which Kinnock had
to fight every inch of the way to keep his soft left supporters on
side, the Militant organisation inside Labour was finally beheaded.
The public were appalled at the ferocity but admired the outcome
and the man who achieved it.

But Kinnock's fight was not just an ideological one. He
and the closely knit team around him, including later Cabinet
ministers Charles Clarke, Patricia Hewitt and John Reid, targeted
the organisational state of the Labour Party as well. On their
watch, the humiliating 1983 campaign shambles was never to be
repeated. Fresh blood was imported into the party's Walworth
Road headquarters. With a mere two-vote majority of the National
Executive Committee backing me, I was recruited as Labour's new
campaigns and communications director and charged with making
a root and branch overhaul of the party's presentation.

But apart from the fact that the party's ruling body was far
from united in backing this communications revolution, there were
other, more basic, obstacles to it, notably the party's policies and
continued yearning for the language and temperament of its past.
And even if the appetite for change had been stronger, there was
also the small matter of my own qualifications for the job. I was
32 years old and since leaving university I had worked in the
TUC economic department, led the British Youth Council and
become a Shadow Cabinet researcher. Hardly the stuff of media
and marketing genius. True, I worked in television prior to my
application for the job but this was a relatively short spell on ITV's
cerebral current affairs programme, *Weekend World*. I had neither
journalistic flair nor advertising talent.

I was fortunate, therefore, that, within days of my appointment,
through a mixture of luck and coincidence, a rather ragged,
long-haired ex-advertising executive who had decided to turn
himself into a US-style political consultant, almost literally turned

up on my doorstep. In fact, it was my *Weekend World* friend Robin Paxton's doorstep on which Philip appeared. He and his future wife, Gail, had known Robin at university and now desperately wanted to be introduced to Labour's new, fresh-faced young campaign director.

Philip arrived at our meeting nervous and jabbering and clutching an eleven-page job application which he thrust into my hand. By the end of our discussion, I had no idea how I would employ him but I knew I would be a fool not to. His enthusiasm seemed boundless. I needed an expert; I also wanted a friend. In Philip, I found both.

Digesting me at that time was an uphill struggle for the party but to take on someone like Philip as well, direct from the world of advertising and PR, was going to be harder still. Not for the last time in the job, I reverted to subterfuge. I persuaded the general secretary, Larry Whitty, that Philip was doing nothing more than a couple of months' consultancy to take stock of our communications and guide us in our future work.

It was the best £600 I ever spent. From that moment until the temporary break-up of our team before the 1992 general election, he and I barely left each other's side. The division of roles was neat – he the man of ideas, me the man of steel, as he liked to call it: while I manned the media barricades, managed the National Executive and the politicians, and helped Kinnock in his fight against Militant, Philip started his private polling and focus group reports, supplied campaign memos and organised a growing army of backroom volunteers from advertising agencies and the like to help us navigate our way back to power. They were called the Shadow Communications Agency, SCA for short. Some had been trying for years to contribute their time and skills to Labour for free. Ignored or rejected, we now added them into the mix of additional people Philip identified and recruited from outside the party.

If, during that time, one thing irked me about Philip, it was his ability never to make enemies. He never lost this knack, under one leader to the next. While I was having to take people on, high and low, inside and outside the party, Philip remained sweetness and light to everyone he met. He buttered up my fellow Walworth Road directors, Joyce Gould and Geoff Bish, befriended my staff and got on terrifically well with the Leader's Office. Why couldn't I manage this conjuring trick?

Barely on top of everything I was having to do, as our first six months wore on, I was becoming more and more worried and sleepless. Changing the Labour Party was like draining a swamp, demanding not just organisational but cultural and attitudinal change on a big scale. Neither of us, when we started, had realised how difficult this would be, and the mountain of public antagonism and distrust the party would have to climb even to get back into contention. But whereas I felt overwhelmed by the task in those early months, Philip was clearly beginning to thrive on it.

The Shadow Communications Agency Rides to the Rescue

Early success saved the day. We knew that amongst the few who were let into the secret of what we were doing – notably Kinnock himself – expectations were high. Having been very critical of the party's campaign efforts since Kinnock took over – the usual avalanche of untargeted charters, ten-point plans, dreary stickers, leaflets and the like – we were charged with delivering a campaign to promote our social policies that needed to be very different. And indeed it was different. Labour's campaign for Freedom and Fairness was translated into *Labour – Putting People First* and comprised simple, hard-hitting messages and campaign materials that were designed and executed with a sharpness and professionalism that the party had not seen for years. The campaign was brought to life by a young girl photographed for the front of the campaign pack reaching up to a blue sky – and who was then held aloft in person by Kinnock at the campaign's launch. This was held with great swagger at the International Press Centre rather than at the usual press conference venue of the boardroom at Walworth Road. The whole event made a tremendous impact, not only on the public who sat up and noticed, thanks to the media attention, but also on our own party members and supporters who felt that at long last we were beginning to compete with the Tories on equal terms (an exception was the MP and NEC member Eric Heffer, who arrived uninvited and stood at the back of the press conference complaining loudly that this was not the Labour Party he joined).

Philip, especially, knew that up to this point he had been on probation. He had talked a big game in his original communications stock take and he had to deliver. Together, this is what Philip and I, and Patricia Hewitt in Kinnock's office, and other party staff like Colin Byrne, Jim Parish, Anna Healy and Jackie Stacey and Andy McSmith, started doing, with great elan. If it had been left either to the party headquarters or to the leader's office alone to organise, it would not have worked so well and Philip provided a highly proficient bridge between the two.

What I learned from Philip and the SCA at this time looks rudimentary now but, back then, we existed in a party environment that lacked the discipline of listening to the voters and understanding them, and then addressing them in language they understood and could identify with. We tried to root every decision in our communications, big and small, in our voter research so as to help rebuild the party's credibility and win back trust. Nowhere was this more important than in economic policy and matters of tax and spending.

Being brutally honest in conveying the findings of our voter research, drawing tough conclusions and converting these into hard-hitting political interventions was difficult. It relied, first, on our political masters wanting to hear the truth and then having the collective political will to agree and implement what flowed from it. In such a complicated 'voluntary' organisation like a political party, this is always harder than outsiders realise. In reality, this did not happen adequately in those early years mainly because it seemed, and probably was, too difficult politically to confront the party and the trade unions with just how far they needed to go to stem our unpopularity. They did not like losing, but nor could they really come to terms with what had to change in order to win.

Following the launch of that original *Putting People First* campaign in April 1986, the newspapers gave us lavish praise. The *Financial Times* greeted 'Mr Kinnock's new party', the *Daily Telegraph* talked of Labour 'shedding its weary cloth cap image', the *Guardian* celebrated Labour's 'political rehabilitation', the *New Statesman* generously conceded the new style might pick up votes and the *Tribune* said that 'this could just be the campaign that wins Labour the next general election'.

Of course, it was no such thing. It was the start of a presentational makeover, nothing more, a bit like our *Investing in People* campaign later in the autumn which featured not just Philip's wife, Gail, but his daughters, Georgia and Grace, in the photo shoots of 'ordinary families' (this campaign also marked the entry of a young *Mirror* journalist, Alastair Campbell, who came into my office one Saturday morning to rewrite the words). But, in all this frenetic activity, as in the following year's general election campaign in 1987, garlanded with its red roses and all its glitz and razzmatazz, and notwithstanding Kinnock's moving oratory, we were applying a spray-paint job to the Labour Party, not re-engineering it. *Private Eye* summed up our 1987 efforts as 'Labour's brilliant election defeat'. We had projected the youthful vigour of Kinnock so strongly throughout the campaign, including in Hugh Hudson's cinematic triumph, because the rest of the party and its policies were largely unchanged. It was the product, not the packaging, where we had to focus next.

It's the Policies, Stupid

Philip claims in his book that he first used the term 'New Labour' some time after the 1987 election, arguing that cosmetic change was insufficient and that we needed to offer proof that we really had learned the lessons of our three electoral defeats since 1979. I suspect Philip did give birth to 'New Labour' because it summed up everything he was arguing at the time. All our research indicated that the public would resist coming home to Labour until we were not just united as a party but unified round policies they saw as relevant and practical. No matter how 'brilliant' our campaigning, it could not compensate for policies that the public believed would leave them financially worse off and, as was the case in unilateral disarmament, defenceless.

Our answer to these stark facts of life was the Policy Review, convened jointly by the NEC and the Shadow Cabinet and consisting of their members. This became our top priority. It was preceded by an SCA presentation called *Labour and Britain in the 1990s* which Philip oversaw with Patricia Hewitt and another SCA volunteer, Deborah Mattinson. This was designed to bring home some essential social and political facts of life to the assembled members – 'another load of bloody rubbish', as inimitable Dennis Skinner shouted when we got the presentation underway.

Once underway, the Policy Review toiled diligently for 18 months, receiving papers, drawing up statements and trying to make some imaginative leaps forward. Unilateralism was despatched with the sort of difficulty that a dentist would have extracting teeth without an anaesthetic. But at least it was done. Trade union law reform was similarly dealt with but only after the youthful Tony Blair, newly appointed as shadow employment secretary, took the bull by its 'closed shop' horns and sent it flying.

In other areas, notably tax and spending, progress was a lot harder. Labour hated Mrs Thatcher's tax-cutting agenda. When the Chancellor, Nigel Lawson, cut the top rate from 60p to 40p, Labour thought many Christmases had arrived early. It was assumed that nobody but the very rich would endorse such unfairness. In fact, the public adjusted rather quickly, as they did again when Norman Lamont introduced his further tax-cutting budget before the 1992 election.

The problem for Labour was that most in the party saw tax as a good in itself and something that was desirable to bring about a more equal society. As Philip kept on explaining to anyone who would listen, the public do not see tax in this way. They regard it as a burden, to be kept to a minimum, cut as much as possible and certainly not frittered away on wasteful projects and indulgences by central or local government and nationalised industries.

As the Policy Review ploughed on through voluminous papers prepared by the policy directorate at Walworth Road, Philip and I became more and more despairing. We had already become targets for some likely and more unlikely people. Roy Hattersley, to whom I thought I was close, had gone on television and spoken of equality and a freer society as the Labour Party's 'Sermon on the Mount', not to be abandoned because 'marketing men' – or 'filofax socialists' as T&G leader Ron Todd called us – found it wasn't attracting 'the trendy, upwardly-mobile middle classes'. Frankly, these were precisely the people Philip and I thought we should be reaching out to. Later, the trade union leader Rodney Bickerstaffe joined in: 'we cannot hand Labour over to marketing men to be packaged like breakfast cereal; our policies cannot be contracted out to the pick of the polls'. This sentiment was beginning to catch on. Rightly, Kinnock saw these statements as shots across his bow and as the catcalls grew, he started to become more unsure of himself and withdrawn.

Despite all our presentational efforts, it was clear that the party was not really cutting into the entrenched mistrust that continued to hold back our poll ratings. It was not only our past divisions, the still fresh memories of Tony Benn's highly symbolic challenge (and near win) for the deputy leadership and the public campaign against the Militant tendency. It went deeper. Voters saw Labour as wedded to public spending and the public sector above all else, to the detriment of the national finances and private enterprise. They were unsure where we stood on the market economy. They identified us with old-style industry and smokestack chimneys. Whereas Mrs Thatcher was seen as committed to a necessary overhaul of the economy whilst oblivious to the social consequences of this, Labour was regarded as the opposite – dedicated to social protection without realising what change the economy had to undergo.

By 1989, two years on from our third election defeat, Philip was insistent that unless the public saw a genuinely new Labour Party taking shape we would be unable to capitalise on the Tories' growing divisions and unpopularity in the ways we wished.

We approached that year's European Parliament elections as a make-or-break moment. Instead of a routine national campaign, with the now highly professional but increasingly familiar offerings of the SCA, we decided to use the Policy Review itself as the centrepiece. Kinnock was understandably concerned that if we launched it in the middle of the campaign it might set off an uncontrollable spate of vote-losing internal argument with the trade unions and the left constituency parties. I was adamant that we needed to risk all, using Philip as usual to provide the evidence and argument needed to overcome Kinnock's reluctance.

Meet the Challenge, Make the Change, the title of the Policy Review publication, may not seem very clamorous or radical by New Labour standards, but the media briefing around the message was clear: Labour was facing a clear injunction to break with the past.

Philip put it bluntly in a memo. He wanted people's idea of Labour to reflect the following statements:

- Labour has changed. Neil Kinnock has delivered a New Labour Party.
- I trust Labour to form a government.
- Labour has sensible economic policies and the team to run them.
- Labour understands people like me.

Meet the Challenge had many policy limitations but we succeeded in making it break through as a major news story. The narrow line we trod was reflected in the accompanying *Aims and Values* statement designed to be a testament to our modernised thinking. It was Kinnock's equivalent to Tony Blair's 'Clause IV' moment less than a decade later.

The inevitable compromises contained in *Aims and Values* summed up where we had got to and how much further we had to travel. We inserted into the text the words describing our economic approach as 'markets wherever possible, government wherever necessary'. By the standards of the day it was trail-blazing. But seeing the trap, the left group on the NEC proposed at the end of the meeting that the words of Clause IV, part 4 (the part of Labour's constitution voicing support for state ownership of the economy's commanding heights) should also be included in the text.

My heart sank and I caught Kinnock's eye. I knew what Philip's focus groups would make of such a fudge. But, in that brief moment, Kinnock and his supporters could not see a way to block the move. I scribbled him a quick note. 'Under no circumstances must it form part of the actual text – I'll print it on the inside cover when we publish the final version and in the meantime put the existing agreed text out to the media after the meeting.' And that's what happened.

The overall effect of the Review was positive or, to put it another way, the hype was desperate but it worked. We went into our first national polling lead since before the 1987 general election and took 14 European Parliament seats off the Tories, exceeding anyone's expectations.

1989 was the peak of Kinnock's electoral achievement. We managed to persuade ourselves that we were finally on our way, with a modern, forward-looking party and policies born of reality and deep values rather than leftist postures.

The False Dawn

So, why in the end didn't all these efforts put us into power? High unemployment, worsening public services, poll tax riots, deep divisions over Europe. Why, despite these political advantages, were our rising polling numbers built on sand? There were three reasons, two political and the third organisational.

Fundamentally, we were projecting Labour in ways the party itself did not believe in. Every policy shift, however small, was stretched by us to mean more than it was. I went through the final Review document with a pen to sharpen every nuance and add every gloss possible to make the public feel we were changing more than we were. I had got used to this, having insisted from the outset of my time at Walworth Road on the right to sign off all printed documents as we, on my side of the shop, were in charge of 'communications'. You can understand why we were so popular with our policy comrades. I had earlier taken this prerogative to within an inch of my life when, in reprinting the party membership cards – they were, after all, a form of communication – I 'forgot' to include the infamous words of part 4 of Clause IV of our constitution. Rightly or not, Larry Whitty ordered the cards to be pulped and reprinted with the magic words duly included (the cost was taken off my budget as a sort of fine).

In certain policy areas, we managed some genuine shifts, for example on home ownership and, as I have said, on defence and trade union law. In the case of the privatisation of the utilities, which Kinnock had originally said he would oppose with every last breath in his body, we said, on Gordon Brown's insistence, that they 'would not be a priority' for renationalisation in view of the costs involved. It was a compromise that did not impress the public who had enjoyed buying and reselling their shares and who, in any case, saw utilities as more commercial than social services. And so it went on, two steps forward, one step back, as we saw later with John Smith's shadow budget in the run-up to the 1992 election. Tax and spending remained our Achilles' heel. As a result, we failed to convince. We were newish but not unambiguously new.

The second reason for the false dawn was Kinnock himself. It is difficult even now to tell what happened but I think he became exhausted by the sheer, constant uphill struggle of forcing his fractious party to follow him without argument or dissent. He was caught in a bind: he craved public support and respect, yet felt that, to remain true to himself, he had to maintain his 'socialist' credentials in ways that the public would not vote for. The great Welsh orator, who had used words to cover this divide and sweep both party and public along with him, suddenly found that the words were no more, or at least, not enough. As Philip said, the well was dry. From then on, Kinnock went into a form of decline, never quite rediscovering the edge and passion he needed to stir the public. The consequences of this were inevitable. As we went into the 1992 election, despite our successes in wrong-footing the Tories over the NHS (winning the Monmouth by-election on a campaign to save the local hospital from 'opting out' of the NHS as a result of Tory reforms), too many voters said they just didn't see Kinnock as Prime Minister. For all his gladiatorial flourishes in Prime Minister's Questions, they had begun to see him more as a manager than a leader, more a consensual front-man for his party than someone who was taking risks in shaping and leading it. Once that feeling starts to settle like concrete, it becomes fatal. The party, in Parliament and amongst the trade union leaders, sensed this was happening but decided not to do anything about it.

This was not the only reason we lost that election. Philip chronicled how the switch from Thatcher to Major, a softer, more unifying figure, signalled to voters that the Conservatives were becoming a gentler, more middle-of-the-road party. But the main issue remained the economy. The country was heading into recession. You might think the incumbent government would have been punished. But the bigger thought was that Labour was still not trusted and that we might make things worse. The Tory machine knew which button to push and they pressed down hard on 'tax and spend'. If times were hard and likely to get harder, could the country afford to spend more, and could any family afford to pay higher taxes? Philip was clear in his warnings of what the electoral consequences of our policies would be. Kinnock heard and he was worried. But others refused to listen as Philip found his ability to guide and cajole the party leadership waning. I have doubted the old adage that 'governments lose elections, Oppositions don't win them' ever since.

But the reason why Philip was holding less sway was my fault. I had decided some years before that I wanted to try my hand at being selected to fight a Labour seat, to forge out on my own, to see whether I could pull it off as a front-of-house performer rather than backroom boy. Philip had been amongst the first of my colleagues I told of my intention. I broke the news over lunch near his office in Soho and he was simultaneously appalled and kind in his encouragement. I could see a sort of agony spreading across his face as he realised the consequences of my being selected and ceasing to be his anchor in our electoral machine.

And so it had come to pass, thanks to Hartlepool. It need not have led to the breaking apart of the machine in the way it did, but this is what happened as the party approached the 1992 election. Of course, at a personal level, I tried to keep close to Philip but because of silly personality rivalries at play, he was under a heavy injunction to keep his distance and not to involve me in the election preparations – a rehearsal of the schism that was to repeat itself when I was forced to leave Tony Blair's government ahead of the 2001 election. It grew more and more difficult for him as he tried in vain to keep together the component parts of the election team. The SCA became more shadow than agency. Campaign decisions began to be taken in two competing camps, one largely unknown to the other. Key frontbench media performers were often excluded. In the 1987 election we might have been on a hiding to nothing but at least we went down in glorious defeat. In 1992, we never fired on all cylinders.

Philip left that election feeling wretched and despondent. He felt a huge ton of responsibility even though he was never actually appointed, let alone elected, to any formal role from beginning to end. I think he preferred it this way, keeping his head down in the personality battles, without it making a difference to his effectiveness. He got by through sheer dint of personality and the natural authority that comes to somebody with his intelligence, charm and prodigious output.

Following the election defeat, he used his time alone to good effect. He went to America and came back with the story of Bill Clinton's strategic brilliance at building a New Democrat coalition that spanned the centre-left of his party and then captured the centre ground of US politics, allowing him dramatically to unseat a one-term Republican President.

It was an extraordinary achievement by Clinton, brought about with discipline and meticulous attention to detail, and one in which Philip, of course, revelled. He brought the key Clinton strategists and campaign directors to meet us in London. He shared the good news with anyone who would listen. He played no meaningful part in John Smith's leadership, preparing, in his mind, for the longer game. That game came to him sooner than he and any of us expected. Philip Gould's finest hour was fast approaching.

'Our Kind of Politics'

David Miliband

5

The last time I saw Philip was a couple of weeks before he died. He was in his favourite place for thinking and talking, on the green sofa on the first floor of his house, his by now very thin legs wrapped around each other, his body arching back and then thrusting forward to make a point, his feet resting on the coffee table in front of him. He was philosophical, funny, passionate, pragmatic – all the things that made him a wonderful friend and colleague.

We had been having these kinds of conversations for 16 or 17 years. As always, his remarkably fertile mind was scanning the intellectual, economic, social as well as political horizon. We covered life, death, children, the NHS, Britain, America, the Middle East. He wanted me to know he had thought through his funeral, and had meticulously planned his gravesite in Highgate Cemetery. And of course we talked about people too.

For Philip, the personal was political in a profound way. His own upbringing – suburban Sidcup, his Dutch mother, failing the 11-plus, Sussex University in the 1960s, professional success through hard work – was his political compass. He saw this first of all in terms of class. The people he met, the sons and daughters of skilled working-class or lower-middle-class parents, were his weathervane. And a clue to his success as a political consultant was that this group was from the 1960s to the 1990s the rising class in British life – rising in terms of numbers, education and influence.

Philip's background was not the same as mine. My family was more middle class; also I had lived in Leeds for four formative years of my life and had a perspective from outside the South. My background was more policy; his more presentation. We were born in different generations. We came at problems from different angles. We didn't agree on everything. But our passions met – a hatred of losing elections to the Tories, a belief in the power of education to help people realise their potential, a commitment to linking politics to ideas.

Towards the end of the meeting, Philip stopped short and said: 'You know, there's never been a better time for our kind of politics.' It felt like an injunction to action as well as a statement of belief. So his comment is the focus of this chapter. In particular, what he meant by 'our kind of politics' – and what kind of progressive politics that is right for the times. After all, the European left has been distinguished for losing elections, not winning them, in the last few years.

Philip was sometimes criticised for a focus on political tactics. He did pioneer for Labour a seriousness of purpose when it came to listening to the electorate. One of the biggest divisions in politics is between people who blame the voters when they lose elections, and politicians who blame themselves. Philip never blamed the voters. He respected voters enough really to try to understand their views. He was not ashamed of focus groups. He saw this as part of democracy. When people said they cared about immigration, or welfare fraud, or crime, he said he wanted to understand their concern, even when he disagreed – sometimes violently – with their views.

He also wanted to know about people's lives. The great sociologist Professor Zygmunt Bauman talks about a big shift in advanced industrialised societies. It starts with the nineteenth- and twentieth-century notion of communities or countries as 'societies of producers', where identity was profoundly shaped by work, and the social life and family life as well as the economic life that was bound up in it. This is the world that reached its political apogee after the 1945 election. But Bauman argues that today the societies of producers have been fragmented or destroyed. So we have become 'societies of consumers', where the shaping of identity comes from a far wider range of sources which are chosen by individuals.

Philip wanted politicians to understand these kind of changes. He thought political tactics needed to emerge from an understanding of society, not vice versa. He also knew that our agenda needed to fight behind enemy lines, and not just on our home territory. He knew, for example, there is nothing Conservatives hate more than having to defend their record on crime. And there is nothing they like more than upstaging us on the fight against inequality – just remember how the 1992 budget with its new 20p rate of income tax completely scuppered Labour's claim to be the party of the poor and the middle.

Strategy and Meaning

But our kind of politics is not primarily about tactics. It is about strategy and meaning. 'Our kind of politics', in Philip's mind, was never meant to be sectarian. But neither was it inchoate. It came together after the end of the Cold War in the 1990s. In Britain it meant a version of progressive politics which bridged historic divides in progressive politics – divides which had kept us out of power and handed large parts of the twentieth century to the Tories.

The first great divide is between people who consider themselves (small l) liberals and those who see themselves as social democrats or socialists. The former put the premium on individual freedom in a market economy; the latter on collective action to achieve social justice. When it works well, progressive politics brings these people together – to outlaw discrimination on ground of colour or creed and thereby promote equality, or to create a welfare state that protects people when they are sick or unemployed and thereby retain their dignity and economic liberty. But the two strands of thought are different, and not always consistent.

In Britain these two parts of the progressive tradition have found their primary home in two different parties – Labour and Liberal. The net result was to let the Tories in for 75 of the last 110 years. In the 1980s it almost destroyed the Labour Party. In truth, the liberal–communitarian axis crosses the left–right axis in politics. Philip was on the communitarian left when it came to crime and welfare, on the liberal centre when it came to economics, and the liberal left when it came to personal social mores and political reform.

So there is complexity in the relationship of liberals to social democrats. Keir Hardie wouldn't have been surprised that Nick Clegg and his colleagues have bought into Tory economics with zeal and enthusiasm; after all, he left the Liberal Party because he despaired of it helping working people. But the truth is that a Labour Party that positions itself in the left-authoritarian box of centralised and statist machine politics does not do justice to itself, or give itself the chance of winning elections.

This is as much about culture as policy, and the way we see political change. This is the second great divide.

It concerns politics as a parliamentary process and politics as mass movement. The two should go together. At their best they do. But the dominant impression from the twentieth century is that parliamentarians have found it difficult to connect their work to mass movements – after all, parties have a small percentage of the population as members – and those outside have been disappointed by achievements in Parliament.

It is ironic that my dad should have written a book called *Parliamentary Socialism*. People often say that his book was about the failure of Labour to be as left-wing as it should be. They often ask what he would have thought of his sons being to the right of him. But the book is not simply a call for Labour to move to the left. The first line is actually about the divorce between parliamentary activity and the development of a movement outside: 'Of all political parties claiming socialism to be their aim, the Labour Party has always been one of the most dogmatic – not about socialism, but about the Parliamentary system.' His denunciation of 'Labourism' was as much about the narrow interpretation of political change as it was about its position on the left–right spectrum.

The truth is that good organisation is necessary to get elected. But the metaphor of the machine summons up an image of cogs.

When people are seen as cogs it produces unhealthy results. And attempts to secure lasting change without popular consent and participation are doomed to failure. Machine politics in the Labour Party has been used as much to throttle the movement and win internal battles as to win the election of Labour to majority in Parliament.

My view, I think Philip's view, is that in the modern age of mass and personalised communication and choice, you cannot have an effective election-winning machine without a living, breathing movement for change. The lack of the openness and dialogue inherent in this vision crippled Labour in the later Blair and Brown years. The failure to reform the party after 1997 was an enduring problem for the task of 'renewal'.

The third great divide is related to the first two, but is distinct. It concerns idealism and realism. This divide has been the bane of the history of the Labour Party.

Anyone who joins the Labour Party, and the vast majority of the people who vote for it, know that in some deep way they are making a commitment not just to their own betterment but also to a better society.

The struggle for the minimum wage is a good example of the struggle between idealism and realism throughout Labour's history. It was a founding demand of the Labour Representation Committee. It was opposed for large parts of the twentieth century by the trade union movement who wanted to maintain a commitment to free collective bargaining – which delivered more to some parts of organised working people, but left others, disorganised, to be exploited. It was the subject of a demonising campaign by the Tories before 1997 – neutered by the decision to put the setting of the rate in the hands of the independent Low Pay Commission. And now, with idealism and realism combined, the Tories who opposed it for 100 years keep saying how much they support it.

The idealism means that no one in the Labour Party is ever satisfied – after all, the 1945 Labour government was denounced for timidity. It's not a bad thing to always want more. It fuels ambition and hope. But the other side of the coin – the betrayal thesis that is rolled out for internal party reasons after every defeat to suggest that the problem was an abandonment of the true faith – is corrosive. It produces scepticism and cynicism.

The truth is that idealism is the oxygen of politics, but realism is its anchor. You need both. Voters, especially poorer ones, cannot afford to let go of reality. They need to pay the bills. But without the vision for a different future, cynicism sets in.

Labour wins when it offers both. The 1945 manifesto offered the vision of a green and pleasant land, tempered by the realities of a war-torn economy, and administered by people who had proved their ability (and patriotism) under the stress of war. The 1964 election campaign offered a new boost to the economy through science, not through nationalisation, overseen by skilled technocrats. In 1997 Labour offered 'a start not a revolution', driven forward by a post-war baby-boom generation. And in each case the offer was about more than policy. It was about culture and ethos. In 1945 it was about a new start – and no return to the 1930s. In 1964 it was about meritocracy. In 1997 it was about openness and social justice.

These three divides explain a lot about the frustration of politics, and the new direction that Labour embraced after 1994. But there is something else. Our kind of politics didn't fit into a neat left/ right categorisation.

The left in the party has over the years stood for nationalisation, for public spending, for women's rights, for unilateral nuclear disarmament, for reforming the state, for equality which was read as equality of outcome. The right has stood for social conservatism, for Atlanticism, for being anti-European (under Gaitskell) and for being pro-European (under John Smith), for the minimum wage, for fiscal prudence and for equality as read as equality of opportunity.

The Labour Party I joined in the 1980s presented every member with a false choice: on the one hand stood Militant and Tony Benn; on the other, the right-wing machine. Neither did justice to my kind of politics. I want to be for equal rights and for fiscal responsibility; for reforming the state and for being pro-European; for equal opportunity in and of itself, and as essential to address inequalities of outcome.

We need our kind of politics now to avoid a false choice of left and right in the party. It is a third way within the party: not the posturing of the left nor the conservatism of the right. And that is the position from where Labour's renewal is coming today. You see it, for example, from leaders in local government who are working to do better for their communities with less money to spend. Each requires us to find the sweet spot of politics that is beyond left and right in the party, and thereby unites the majority of the party.

The Economic Crisis as Turning Point

That strategic positioning now needs to be applied in highly distinctive circumstances. The financial crisis of 2007/08 in western industrialised economies cost thousands of billions of dollars and hundreds of thousands of jobs. It was a massive market failure, and a massive regulatory failure. It was the acute symptom of a chronic shift in the balance of economic power around the world. You cannot have the worst economic crisis in 80 years and expect politics to carry on as before.

China is creating a new economy the size of Greece every twelve and a half weeks, and an economy the size of Spain every 16 months. The four BRIC countries (Brazil, Russia, India and China) are creating new economic wealth the size of Italy – the eighth largest economy in the world and the fourth largest population in Europe – every year. UN estimates are that 50 million people a year from Asia will join the global middle class (incomes $6–18,000 a year) every year – precisely at the time when the growth of the western middle class has gone into reverse.

In truth, neither left nor right of the political spectrum has yet shown the strategic intellectual imagination to respond to this shock to the system. The right has reached for austerity – a pre-Keynesian fetish for shrinking government spending whatever the circumstances. The left has struggled to turn anger into answers.

For the left, the danger is a scissors effect which, if we are not careful, will slice us in half. Austerity economics and austerity politics are pulling in different directions – when in the 1990s economics and politics pointed in the same direction. Warmed-up 1990s social democracy will not provide a strategy for government in these circumstances.

The economics calls for short-term expansion and medium-term contraction, but the politics in Europe at least is biased towards the opposite. The economics calls for tighter international coordination, yet the politics is rebelling against governance that is less accountable and further away. The economics calls for more open flows of labour, not least to cope with Europe's demographic challenge, yet the politics is more nativist than internationalist. The economics says job growth (not productivity growth) is going to be in predominantly public sectors of health, care and education, but the politics of taxation makes expansion difficult. The economics says 'the world is flat', but the politics is more and more local – witness the debate in Scotland about going independent.

Perhaps the toughest tension is the following. The economics calls for new public investment focused on developing new economic capacity, from green energy to new sciences, and demography demands a focus on new social needs, like eldercare. But the politics of tough times make it especially hard to shift away from longstanding programmes that support the poor, the old or the sick (about half of total UK public spending). This is especially tough for the centre-left. On the one hand we need and want to do justice to the legacy of twentieth-century achievement, above all the achievement of the post-war Keynesian welfare state, where government took responsibility through fiscal policy for levels of demand and employment in the economy, and through public services and the welfare state for making life civilised and worthy of a relatively rich country. In my constituency I know how much difference these gains still make to people's lives.

At the same time, we know that there are new needs as well as new pressures. These come from demography, the resource crunch, stagnating living standards, changing family structures, migration. We simply cannot fund 35-year retirements out of funds designed for an average of 15 years. We cannot sustain childcare and eldercare and healthcare and education out of a revenue base designed for two of the four. In policy terms we believe the changes in the past were right, but know that new needs cannot just be piled on old structures of funding and delivery. In political terms, we need the support of those in the bottom third of the income distribution who are the main beneficiaries of the welfare state, while recognising that social and economic change means that no longer creates a winning coalition. As Peter Kellner brutally points out: in the 1950s, most people were not taxpayers, but now they are.

I therefore think Ed Miliband and Ed Balls are right to emphasise the need to return to prudence in fiscal policy. Credibility is easy to lose and hard to regain. We have some very difficult choices ahead about how to balance the poverty of those short-changed in the Tory years with the need to invest in the wealth-creating potential of the economy in the future. The crash has raised the bar for fiscal policy.

The challenge we face is intellectual and political. Intellectual about how state, market and citizen relate to each other in western societies suffering unprecedented economic challenge; political about how centre-left parties fashion national stories in a context of fragmented societies. The financial crisis has blown a massive hole in the right's thesis about efficient markets. The sovereign debt crisis has resurrected the 1970s debate about the fiscal crisis of the state. The combination has left the electorate turning away from mainstream parties of centre-right and centre-left.

Labour Cannot be Conservative

My perspective is that Labour cannot afford to be the conservative party – defending the status quo without a big agenda for the future. Sure, 'Blue Labour' is right to warn against believing that all change is progressive. It isn't when it strips out human values in the name of progress. The centre-left succeeds when it acts in concert with the most dynamic currents in economy and society in the name of advancing human values.

In the modern world, all over the world, that revolves around three sets of issues – all of them taking on new meaning after the crash.

The first is about how to protect people – and how people can protect each other – from modern risks. I am thinking of economic and financial risks, but also wider. This debate can take you into economic protectionism – but I think that is the wrong response. Instead, I think it is about pooling insurance against risk in a way that includes the whole of society; establishing a strategic view of government that is not cluttered by confusion between ends and means; and I think the Labour leadership are right to seek to develop, popularise and own an agenda of responsible capitalism – responsible because it seeks to curb unaccountable power, capitalism because it is serious about wealth creation. There are a number of critical issues on the latter, from training to industrial policy, but we also need to get ahead of the curve on issues like ownership. I don't mean the balance of public and private ownership; the Ownership Commission makes the point that the balance *within* private ownership – where the plc is the super-dominant form – is wrong, leaving our economy far less balanced and resilient than our competitors'.

The second is how to strengthen community in an age of massive change. This raises tough issues, notably about migration which loomed large in our election and even larger in France. But it also asks questions about the fundamental social bargain and its legitimacy – which, as we saw in the 2011 riots, is fragile and brittle.

Both these sets of issues have been getting a good political airing. But the third hasn't. It is about how people can have more control over their own lives. While there has been a lot of talk about the radical wave of democratisation that has been seen in the

Middle East, there has not been much reflection on the sense of disempowerment that people feel in western countries – not just from the political process, but from key decisions that affect their lives, in public services and beyond.

This sense of disempowerment is economic – on issues from debt to training to pensions. It applies to social policy – for example, on issues of crime, where victims continue to feel the system doesn't listen. It is a real issue in public services – not least because the more parents and patients are involved in education and health, the more successful and productive the services are, and austerity means that there is a squeeze on this kind of outreach. It is painfully true in welfare policy where national rules and complex lives rub up against each other every day. It is true in housing policy, where anyone outside the charmed circle of home ownership is left feeling they have to make do. It comes through strongly on employment policy – where young people not destined for university especially feel that there are neither the options nor the information for them to take charge of their lives. And it is true of politics too, where the majority of voters feel that the political system doesn't work for them.

This sense of disempowerment sits alongside the reality that a more educated and informed citizenry in a more informed society will demand more say over the things that matter to them. The failure of politics, left and right, to speak to this concern, explains a lot about the wide sense of disappointment and disillusion that people have about politics. So the renewal of the centre-left has to speak to the redistribution of power.

It is amazing really that the agendas of 'public service reform' or 'welfare reform' should have been so divorced from issues of governmental reform. But if you think about it, an under-reformed central government is unlikely to be a credible reformer of education or health or the welfare state. In England, London has gained a mayor, but cities lack important powers. This can be the start of how we address the political aspects of the English question (a necessary but not sufficient condition of addressing the social questions).

If you take the redistribution of power as your starting point, you develop an agenda that goes way beyond the reform of government – important though that is. If cities were in charge of shaping welfare-to-work policy for the young unemployed, you would see local coalitions of public, private and voluntary sectors coming together to address what is now seen as a national crisis. As Graeme Cooke has argued in an IPPR pamphlet, since DWP housing benefit policy drives housing expenditure, it is small wonder we don't have a successful housing policy. If parents cannot turn to a local schools commissioner when they feel there is no choice of school for their child, then equity and efficiency are breached. If you recognise that the future sustainability of the health service depends on its integration with social care, then the route to better service and more efficient working by both the health service and local authorities comes into view.

Any future Labour government is going to have to do different with less if it is to tackle the inequities and insecurities that affect modern Britain. The reality of austerity needs to be our spur to radicalism, not to reaction. A good test for policy is whether it puts the power of people alongside the specialism and innovation of professionals and the leadership of government. One of my favourite examples is personalised budgets for disabled people. It is radical in the best sense of the word. That really is our kind of politics.

Conclusion

I am writing this on the train from Newcastle to London, on the way to the interment of Philip's ashes. I think he would have been energised but also challenged by this agenda. The old certainties of the return from political oblivion in the 1990s were not an answer for all time. They need to be renewed.

Philip was concerned that as the world became more open and connected – more democratic – conventional politics was losing its followers. He called this the 'empty stadium' problem. He was right.

This is a remarkable era of democratisation in economic and political (and personal) relationships. Power is shifting from organisations, governments and businesses, to individuals better educated, better informed, better connected and better empowered than ever before. I call this the 'civilian surge'.

Yet it makes representative democracy feel frustrating and clunky at best, and useless and corrupt at worst. Differential turnouts – in Britain, over 75 per cent for the middle and upper class, just over 55 per cent for those at the bottom – are only one aspect of the how political disaffection affects most those who can afford it least.

This means the political model for Labour – its coalition, its way of operating – needs to be comprehensively rethought. Society is too fragmented and politics too dynamic for the model of centralised government 'delivery' to a passive population to have real traction on the inequalities and insecurities that people face. But so too is machine politics utterly inadequate to the electoral and policy challenges we face.

If you think about our recent history, this point becomes obvious. Our problems in the last Parliament were not that we were too far ahead of the electorate when it came to economic and political reform, but that we were left behind. We were too late to an active industrial policy, as good times even after the dot-com bubble burst in 2000/01 blinded us to the fact that we did not have a good system. In the end we were perceived to lack clear direction on issues like crime or education. And tactical machine politics seemed to take over. In this way we invited a backlash, and got one.

I think a lot of the reason comes from the failure to reform the party by opening up its structures. We got cut off from the voters after the 2001 election, even though we won in 2005. I made a speech in 2004 saying that a defeat for the Tories in 2005 would change politics for a long time, by defeating a philosophy not just a party. The result was in fact a warning to both parties – that unless they changed they would be in trouble. But that third victory was better understood by the Tories than by us. The Tories heeded the warning; we didn't. They turned outwards; we turned inwards.

Our kind of politics means seeking out the most dynamic currents in society, and seeking to give them a rocket boost. It means identifying the grain of change – whoever is in government – and seeking to shape it in the service of progressive values. That requires a party open to and connected with the diverse communities it seeks to serve.

It is a huge sadness that Philip is not here to meet this challenge with us. But our kind of politics – his kind of politics – is above all about being ready to rethink in the face of changing facts. That is a vital legacy in the years ahead.

The Land and the Sea

6

James Purnell

Brookwood and Burpham

I remember sitting with Philip on a sunny-bright, lime-green sofa, talking about Blue Labour. He was intrigued by Maurice Glasman, the academic then giving our friends an allergic reaction. He encouraged me:

> You should explore it. It's not my thing – purpose is my thing. But politics is Hegelian – you need to reconcile the opposites. You should explore it.

By 2010, Philip had discarded the hedging and temporising that barnacles most political ideas. He didn't have to persuade anyone any more, he could just push his ideas to adamantine clarity. He was excited about the world, technology, the defenestration of the powerful, the energy of the twenty-somethings.

We grew up in the same corner of Surrey – Brookwood for him, Burpham for me. Four golf courses and two decades separated us. This is where London's commuter belt gives way to the countryside, among what he called the people Labour betrayed.

Terrified by the pressure, 'physically shaking', Philip failed the 11-plus. (That anyone as brilliant as Philip could end up on the wrong side of that premature divide should be the end of the argument over grammar schools.) Philip's childhood tragedy was Labour's electoral saviour. He didn't just respect the views of voters: he viscerally agreed with them. As he said in *The Unfinished Revolution*:

> Whenever I hear people being criticised for their blinkered and reactionary views on crime, or welfare, or aversion to paying taxes, I always ask silently:

have you known the dreadful, repetitive tedium of manual work, not just for the long university holidays, but for life; lived in cramped houses, in communities where walking the streets late at night is not a safe option; known the cancerous insecurity of work as clerks or office administrators, not poor, but never safe, and always worrying about the cost of providing for your family?[1]

The Labour Representation Committee had been founded to express the views of ordinary families in Parliament. By the 1980s, the conversation had been reversed: Labour was now telling ordinary families what they should believe. Philip remembered sitting

in the shadow Cabinet room as the self-interest and materialism that was gripping the electorate in the 1980s was described during a polling presentation. I heard the tut-tutting of disdain from the assembled advisers and officials and thought to myself: you all live in big, comfortable houses, have Tuscan holidays and drive large cars. What do you know about the way ordinary people live?[2]

Trimdon and Islington

What do you know about the way ordinary people live? When I first worked for Tony Blair, in 1990, that was the question he could answer better than any other Labour politician. The argument about the closed shop was still rumbling on, and I remember getting very excited about a poll which showed that even trade union favoured getting rid of it. I rushed into his office with my crucial piece of information, and he just looked at me quizzically – 'of course they oppose it – they disagree with most of what Ron Todd says they believe'.

The received history about Tony Blair's ascent goes like this. Westminster took notice of him when he ditched the closed shop. The public took to him as Shadow Home Secretary, with his 'tough on crime, tough on the causes of crime' slogan, and his speech about community after the Bulger murder. However, that leaves out a couple of important bivouacs on the ascent. There was Andrew Neil putting him on the cover of the *Sunday*

Times magazine in 1992, and – even earlier – the barbecues in his Sedgefield constituency.

In the 1980s, Labour was still struggling to attract voters, let alone members. But one constituency stood out – Sedgefield, his constituency, which had recruited 2,000 members, by letting people pay what they wanted, and making membership a lot more like joining the Working Men's Club, something you just did. Today, Labour is full of active parties (as well as a few in need of defibrillators), but in those days this was so remarkable that *On the Record* (the BBC's flagship politics programme) devoted a show to it. People wanting to join a political party? Looking forward to meetings? Indeed, not having meetings, but enjoying themselves? The revolution might have been far from finished, but it had started.

New Labour was born there, in Trimdon, not Islington. The barbecue guests may have been from the other end of the country to Brookwood but they wanted the same things: low crime, good public services, a decent job, protection for their family. They were patriotic, faithful, knew the importance of good, hard work.

When I first met Maurice Glasman, closer to Islington than Trimdon, he reminded me of those days. He introduced me to London Citizens, the community organisers, whose American sister organisation had trained Barack Obama, and taught him that 'change will come from a mobilized grass roots'.[3] Here were people with jobs outside politics who were still interested in politics. They spoke of the ordinary suffering from which politics grows: people not earning enough; working two, three jobs; never seeing their kids, let alone their partners; being invisible at dusk as the office workers left them to empty the waste paper bins; not invited to the Christmas party; not listened to by any political party.

Trimdon and London Citizens. The politics of ordinary life, rather than abstract concepts or distributional graphs. I sensed that New and Blue flowed from the same source and, that by going back upstream, we could both clarify Labour's approach and get back in touch with the voters who had inspired it.

Not quite what most of my friends thought. 'Populist, anti-immigrant, Europhobic' (Mandelson). 'A Labour equivalent of warm beer and old maids bicycling' (Blair). Most recently, Patrick Diamond and Michael Kenny concede that 'its diagnosis of Labour's ills was powerful', yet argue that 'Blue Labour's remedy may have offered the wrong kind of medicine',[4] and urge Labour to return to its liberal fountainhead, before the bifurcation of the early twentieth century.

I was surprised to see people with whom I agree on so much have the opposite reaction to mine. Previously, in *New Labour's Old Roots*, Patrick Diamond had argued correctly that '"New" Labour isn't really new at all. It has old roots in ethical socialism and revisionist social democracy.'[5] Yet when Blue Labour, essentially a revisionist step within that ethical socialist tradition, appeared, it was treated more as an enemy than a cousin.

Why? Because the Labour Party's modernisers, in each generation, have seen their first task as defeating impossibilist romanticism. And when they glimpsed Blue Labour, they saw that romantic threat, rather than an ideological relative. They are still haunted by the past.

Hardie and Macdonald

This tension in the family also has old roots, going back to Ramsay MacDonald and Keir Hardie, to their uneasy alliance and easy rivalry.

After 1997, Jonathan Powell's desk was squeezed in just outside Tony Blair's infamous sofa-strewn den. If a meeting with the PM started late, advisers like me would hang around just outside the door, often knocking aside a biography of a Labour leader that Jonathan kept to hand. He had a Labour leader's biography on his desk. Anyone less iconoclastic might have opted for Kinnock or Attlee. Jonathan had gone for Ramsay MacDonald.

At the time, I worried what Labour MPs would think if they saw it. But in retrospect, it made a sophisticated historical point.

Because, without Ramsay MacDonald, there would have been no Labour Party, nor indeed a Labour government for him to betray.

In 2006, the Parliamentary Labour Party celebrated its hundredth anniversary. I remember the Labour historian and peer Ken Morgan addressing the PLP, during its weekly Monday evening meeting. He talked about our forebears, about the first meeting of the PLP a hundred years earlier, and about how much of the programme that they had wished for in 1906 had been achieved by the 1997 government. The main exception, teetotalism, wasn't regretted.

We often register the unspoken, half-consciously, a shadow of a question hanging in the air. Looking back at that night, I realise I was asking myself: why then? Why 1906? After all, it was 14 years since Keir Hardie had won West Ham. It was two decades since his mentor Robert Cunninghame-Graham had been elected in North West Lanarkshire. Described by Caroline Benn as 'a fluent linguist, explorer, naturalist, and author, and undoubtedly the most accomplished equestrian ever to enter Parliament',[6] Cunninghame-Graham was Britain's first socialist MP. But after those early triumphs, Labour was a parliamentary disaster. The 1895 general election was as disappointing as it could have been – the 28 candidates of the Independent Labour Party and of the Social Democratic Federation all lost.

The Labour movement faced the classic insurgent party's dilemma – did they cooperate with the established party, or try to replace it? Before 1895, Hardie had (at least in public) mostly promoted rivalry to the Liberals. The rout forced a retreat, to a tactic of cooperate and (hope to) supplant.

Ramsay MacDonald is the hero of 1906. By 1903, the Labour Representation Committee was three years old but struggling at the margins of political life. That January, MacDonald started negotiations with Herbert Gladstone, the Liberal Chief Whip, negotiations which were kept secret from everyone except Hardie, and remained so for many years. The agreement reached in September of that year that the Liberals would give Labour a free run in 30 seats got Labour's 29 MPs elected in 1906.

Hardie was in many ways as pragmatic as MacDonald. Yes, his rhetoric was often sharply anti-Liberal. Having been stitched up and rejected by Liberal associations in his early career, he understood before anyone else that Labour needed its own independent representation – there was no future in Lib-Labbery. His political theory was idealistic, a spiritual, transformative ethical socialism. But when it came to organisation he was a wily, courageous pragmatist, and can claim much of the credit for saving Labour from the cul-de-sacs into which other social democratic movements drove.

If MacDonald is the hero of 1906, then Hardie's year is 1900, and Labour's founding Conference. Hardie's biographer, Caroline Benn, paints the picture: 'socialism's main advocates were SDF delegates who moved bull-at-a-gate to commit the new alliance to a class war' but were 'promptly opposed by trade unionists with their own proposals including one that only working-class men could be chosen to stand'.[7] Faced with ideological socialism and narrow workerism, Hardie saw off both. It was Hardie's motion that defeated both extremes, ensuring the new group would be an independent force representing labour, but not tying its hands on ideology or electoral strategy. That motion allowed Labour to defer all the divisive questions, and provided the base for it to become a majoritarian movement. The SDF offered a schismatic future; the Fabians might have accepted a subordinate one; the trade unions might have excluded the middle classes. Hardie saw off all those threats.

Within the Labour Representation Committee, Hardie was prepared to take a stand. But when it came to national politics, he was too often content to let MacDonald do the deals and take the opprobrium. Here was carved the fault-line in Labour's soul. Idealism or pragmatism? Principles or results? Dreams or reality? All left-wing parties face this tension. People of good judgement can disagree about how to reconcile the two. But reconciled they need to be – without pragmatism, Labour might have suffered the fate of the French left, balkanised into irrelevance for most of the twentieth century. Instead, steered first by Hardie and then by MacDonald, it became the most important social democratic party of the first half of the twentieth century.

But the later years of MacDonald's biography have infected this part of Labour's tradition. His eventual betrayal gave pragmatism his bad name. No subsequent Labour leader would claim his mantle. What should have been a tension, which could create energy, became a choice, which begat traitors.

That shadow still hung over Tony Blair even at his most popular, making his first speech as Labour leader in 1994. Here is the moment just before the Clause IV 'moment':

> Some of you support me because you think I can win. But it is not enough.
>> We are not going to win despite our beliefs.
>> We will only win because of our beliefs.
>> ...
>> There is no choice between being principled and unelectable; and electable and unprincipled.
>> We have tortured ourselves with this foolishness for too long.
>> We should win because of what we believe.

At its best, New Labour attempted to reopen the settled judgement of the Labour tradition that there was an inevitable choice between principle and electability, that there was a principled position which was unelectable, but fixed, and that the task of Labour politics was to work out the minimum sacrifice to electability that needed making on that altar.

Where was that best of New Labour? In policy. That's where pragmatism met idealism. An NHS, better funded, free at the point of use, but where patients had the power. Sure Start, a new common institution supporting aspiration, reducing inequality. Pensions reform, guaranteeing every employee a company pension, and requiring employers to match their contributions. These were policies that were both principled and electable.

New Labour was at its best on policy. To warm up the audience before a leader's speech, we'd show a video of our policies. To win an argument, at the PLP or a CLP, we'd list our policies. To remind voters why they should vote for us, we'd repeat our policies. On policy, we could win because of what we believed.

The Neo-Liberal Tide

But we never won the ideological argument. We didn't convince others that there was a dynamic, ethical argument from which those policies grew. And too often, that was because we hadn't resolved for ourselves what kind of Labour argument it was. Since we weren't clear about our argument, it's no surprise we struggled to convince others too.

In 1994, Labour's recent history was one of defeat and discord, so when we started looking for sources of renewal, we didn't start there. Instead, we looked abroad. For those who had done PPE at Oxford (in other words, most of those involved), the intellectual starting point was often the American liberalism of John Rawls and Amartya Sen. For those who had studied in New England, or liked to holiday there (still, in other words, most of the third way's thinkers), the rhetorical starting point was the Kennedys and Clinton. Although there was much to learn from America, we took collateral damage. We didn't sound like we had much faith in our own tradition.

That left us in a double bind. For voters, we were too Labour. For some activists, we weren't Labour enough. But most of our policies were popular, so we fought the argument there. When activists didn't like a particular policy, we often took a short cut. 'Sorry, the electorate won't buy it.' Or 'Sorry, globalisation.'

But each short cut actually took us away from the real destination – of convincing activists and voters that New Labour was an ethical expression of Labour's values, rather than a necessary compromise with them.

There was another problem: defining ourselves against 'Old Labour'. That rhetorical tactic had worked – it had convinced the voters that Labour had changed. But again there was collateral damage – it created the impression that New Labour was a new party. What for us was revisionism, to others sounded like abandonment. When 'New Labour' sounds to many like 'Not Labour', it becomes difficult to convince them that it flows from Labour's tradition. Even Kinnockite modernisers like Charles

Clarke, when hearing the past denounced as 'Old Labour', thought 'Do they mean me?'

New Labour was confident about policy and politics, but accommodating about the assumptions that underlay both. Those assumptions had been formed in the 1980s, in the battles which Labour had fought but Thatcherism had won: that markets worked most of the time; that we had to be strong on defence; that the City would leave the country if regulated; that the welfare state was only funded on sufferance; that you couldn't win without News International; that the electorate was essentially Conservative. In the 1990s, those assumptions delineated the world of the possible; they were the boundaries of the sensible.

We accepted that those were the touchlines of the political pitch, but then played up and down its left wing: putting up taxes for the NHS, increasing spending on tax credits from £2 billion to £28 billion, reducing child and pensioner poverty. The neo-liberal project had always been to shrink the state; in contrast, we grew it. So we weren't neo-liberals. But nor did we overturn the neo-liberal assumptions that underpinned political debate.

The danger of arguing within your opponents' assumptions is that you win the skirmishes but lose the war. We were doing good Labour things. But we weren't winning a common-sense argument for Labour. Then, when the Labour things stopped being good, when the economy turned down, we didn't have an argument on which to fall back, other than you can't trust the Tories. In contrast, they could bring their common-sense argument out of the drawer: the country was spending beyond its means; the only answer was to cut. Without Labour roots, the saplings of the third way didn't stand a chance when the wind got up.

In the middle of that financial storm, I came across Blue Labour.

Focus Groups and One-to-Ones

I first met Maurice the month that I resigned from the Cabinet: June 2009.

A few months later, I found myself in the Boys' Brigade National Headquarters in Hemel Hempstead discussing power with a nun, a student leader, an evangelical Oxbridge graduate, a Congolese political refugee, a British Ghanaian social worker, and a Muslim ex-civil servant. We were all on the five-day London Citizens training in community organising. Put into pairs, each of us could have found something on which we disagreed violently. But we could also find things on which we agreed. We could leave our views on religion, homosexuality, Iraq, outside the room, and organise around the living wage, for example.

This wasn't a political meeting, but it took me straight back to the practice and spirit in which the Labour Party was founded, finding a way through differences of religion, background and ideology to organise around a common interest: the representation of the people.

Back then, this work had been done in unions, by the *Clarion* newspaper, in Hardie's editorials in the *Labour Leader*, during speech-making tours.

But by the 1990s, the work was being done in focus groups.

Almost everyone misunderstands Philip's groups. Tony says that he often didn't believe them – because they so often seemed to agree with what Philip thought in the first place. But that is to think that Philip was going to Watford to find out what floating voters thought and then report back.

That's not what Philip did. Instead, he went to people's front rooms and argued with them:

> I took my courage in my hand and conducted my first group. No one trained me, I just did it. And I loved it. I loved the direct contact with the electorate, the way that I could put arguments, hear arguments, confront arguments, develop ideas, feel the intensity of a point of view … I do not just see focus groups and market research as a campaigning tools; I see them as an important part of the democratic process: part of a necessary dialogue between politicians and people, part of a new approach to politics.[8]

If the focus group was the organisational unit of New Labour, then for Blue Labour, it's the one-to-one. Two people who don't know each other sit down for the best part of an hour, and talk about what inspires, shapes and hurts them. Like focus groups, one-to-ones are democratic, they create energy, they engage with ideas, but are grounded in experience. They are realistic and emotional, angry and committed. But one-to-ones add two elements: they are about everyone, not just floating voters; and they can start a relationship. If a one-to-one goes well, people keep in touch.

Focus groups and one-to-ones are where Labour can find the confidence to win that ducked ideological battle with Thatcherism. Because they remind us that the Labour tradition wasn't foreign, or theoretical, but grew out of the conversations and compromises of hundreds of thousands of English, Welsh, Irish and Scottish people. That tradition then flows through the words of Hardie and Tawney, the actions of Attlee and Bevan, the policies of 1945 and 1997.

One-to-ones give us confidence that we can win a common-sense argument for Labour. They remind us that with time and relationships, you can build a common interest.

Will one-to-ones bear the weight I am putting on them? Are they really the whole story about how to renew Labour?

No. They're not the whole story. But they are where the story starts, not just organisationally, but philosophically. Tawney put this best, when he said that Labour shouldn't start from 'transcendental doctrines nor rigid formulae but a common view of the life proper to human beings, and of the steps required at any moment more nearly to attain it'.

Why does that matter? Because the starting point matters. It leads us to a different scenery, and different policies. If we take Tawney's goal of 'a life proper to human beings', then the duty of politics becomes helping people reach their dreams and protecting them from what they fear.

New Labour took a huge number of 'the steps required at [that] moment more nearly to attain' that life – from cutting crime to improving parental leave.

But freed of the ideological assumptions of the last 30 years, no longer swimming against the neo-liberal tide, we could go much further. We would continue to support aspiration, but we could be much more open about the need to protect people, and more confident about our ability to do so. In welfare, for example, we would continue to expect people to work, and take a job if offered one. But we would protect people better. We would guarantee that no one would be out of work for more than a year. We would guarantee every employee a company pension. We would guarantee parents properly paid leave and free or affordable childcare. And we would fund that by cutting some of the universal benefits that people value less and which don't protect them.

We would continue to believe in competitive markets. But we wouldn't rely as much on a centralised, elitist economy, concentrated on London and the City. We would think much more deeply about how to stimulate private sector growth all around the country, and about how employees can have power within their company.

We would be proud that New Labour turned around the debate on the state – by both reforming it and increasing spending. But we would ask ourselves whether we had really given citizens power over their public services. About whether they had too often been treated as clients, rather than people. About whether we had given them enough control over how their communities were changing.

Romantics versus Modernisers?

But what about change? Blue Labour appeals to many because it talks about what we want to conserve, whereas New Labour's appeal is that it is brave about change. This is a conversation that is only just starting. It's been hard to have whilst both cousins were insulting each other, decrying each other's nostalgia and change-mania respectively. But it's a conversation about trajectory rather than destination.

One of Blair's greatest achievements was making Britain feel comfortable with change, by convincing us to believe in progress again. That belief can be self-reinforcing – if people believe that there is more to hope for than to fear, they are more prepared to take the risks that will make that happen. They are more tolerant of immigration, more willing to start companies, more ambitious for their families. We shouldn't lose the future by trying but failing to conserve the past.

I would have loved to hear Maurice and Philip discuss this. I know what Maurice would have said, because we discussed it last week: that New Labour ignored institutions, and their ability to shape, slow and then deepen change. Look at the universities, the grammar schools, Parliament, the Labour Party.

Any conversation with Philip was surprising. But here is my guess at what he would have said. Even in 2009, he was predicting the Global Spring. He was excited about how technology and the end of deference were rebalancing power. Once politicians and business leaders had power: today, it is leaking from their hands. New Labour seminars often talked about empowerment. But Philip really believed it was becoming possible, and that we had to reform the state to grab that opportunity.

My answer grows from those two points of view. Government does have a duty to make change possible, to overcome the interests vested in the status quo. But we need to find a way of letting the people decide what that change should be and managing how it happens. That kind of participative democracy once seemed naive. Today, with the pincer movement of new technology and community organising, it seems possible – and if we can create legitimate institutions and powerful individuals, desirable.

New Labour was only just setting out on that journey. We'd started giving power to consumers – but we weren't sure about workers. Citizens could have choice over public services, but not over who was a Lord. And even when we did give people power, we often still wanted to tell them how they should use it, whether because of our centralising instincts, or a distrust of diversity.

The Land and the Sea

Philip used to say that you didn't have a strategy unless it was written down. Though that cost him again and again as his strategy notes got leaked, normally in the middle of general elections, nevertheless he was right. Unless you've written down what you won't do, you can always revert to it, under pressure. Between 1994 and 1997, Labour had a political strategy, and that made it impossible to revert to type on public spending, on bad teaching, on trade union legislation.

People get all sorts of odd ideas about strategy. Sometimes they give it too little content – thinking that vociferously repeating unrealistic ambitions is the same as having a strategy. Sometimes they give it far too much content – detailed plans for everything a government or a campaign will do. But a strategy is really just a game plan – a quite high-level statement of a realistic goal and how to get there.

In 1997, New Labour's strategy was to win a substantial majority, by campaigning on three themes: the many not the few; the future not the past; leadership not drift – all the time reassuring voters that Labour had changed. A strategy of this sort creates some default settings, which allows you to target resources, coordinate actions and agree what you won't do.

That strategy was a great way of winning elections and (for a good few years) a pretty good way of running the country. But, as Philip argued, it 'emerged in reaction to the policy and politics that preceded it ... and it must renew in reaction to the new conditions it has created'.[9]

This chapter has argued that this renewal should take Blue Labour as its reference point, rather than any philosophy one can detect in the coalition. It gives us a double-confidence: first to seek renewal in our own tradition, and second that we can build a common interest with the people, which in turn gives them power.

This is the way to reconcile principle and pragmatism. We are no longer judging ourselves by an abstract idea, decided by an elite, narrowed down to a utilitarian concept of equality. If people have power, both in their lives and through politics, they can decide both how to build a common life, and where to make compromises. They become Hardie and MacDonald at their best. We have inserted them into the paradox, and given them the power to choose, rather than pretended to ourselves it doesn't exist in principle and then acted as if we couldn't convince anyone of our views in practice.

Philip had a richer word for pragmatism: duty. Talking about his parents, he said 'my father gave me duty, my mother idealism. They gave me both the land and the sea.' Pragmatism is a thin word – a calculation you make. Duty is a human word – an obligation you owe to people because you know them; a loyalty to ideas that you found together.

Philip lived this inheritance by mixing a fascination with ideas with a dedication to winning. Focus groups are much more part of Labour's roots of deliberative democracy than was recognised at the time. Of course, Philip had a further genius, of turning those conversations into political strategy, and he would no doubt have done much better than the default settings I've suggested here. But here's my offering for the beginning of a new strategy:

- Progress and protection.
- Giving people and institutions the power to change.
- Deciding together how to stop unnecessary suffering.
- All the time, thinking about how we build a common life together.

A journalist who went to Philip's wake said to me that it had made him not only understand New Labour but think immeasurably better of it. He realised that we were a family, with all the love and compromise, rivalry and shared dreams that go with that.

Blue and New are cousins in that family affair. Their policies spring from an ethical, vibrant Labour argument. They are idealistic and dutiful.

We can indeed have both the land and the sea.

Notes

1. Philip Gould, *The Unfinished Revolution* (Abacus, 2011) p. 10.
2. Gould, *Unfinished Revolution*, p. 10.
3. Barack Obama, *Dreams from my Father* (Canongate, 1995), p. 133.
4. http://www.guardian.co.uk/commentisfree/2012/mar/12/labour-lost-liberal-streak
5. Patrick Diamond, *New Labour's Old Roots: Revisionists Thinkers in Labour's History: 1931–1997* (Imprint Academic, 2004).
6. Caroline Benn, *Keir Hardie* (Hutchinson, 1992), p. 46.
7. Benn, *Keir Hardie*, p. 156.
8. Gould, *Unfinished Revolution*, pp. 322–323.
9. Gould, *Unfinished Revolution*, p. 402.

Philip Gould and the Rise of the Scorekeepers

7

Danny Finkelstein

Towards the end of Philip Gould's life he came to lunch at *The Times*, where I work as a journalist. Afterwards, we headed toward the lift discussing the next election, Philip's favourite topic of conversation. As we stood there waiting for the elevator to arrive, it suddenly struck me that this might be the last conversation of the many we enjoyed. That I might not see him again. So I turned and said. 'Philip, I just want you to know that you have been a great inspiration to me.' He smiled, got in to the lift and the doors shut. I was right. I didn't see him again.

There was something about Philip that prompted you to say such things to him – gauche things that were slightly too forward given how well we knew each other. His openness and honesty were infectious, so you found yourself saying things that you hadn't planned. After lunches with Philip I often found myself wondering – did I really say that out loud?

But the words weren't said because it was a nice way of taking leave of a dying man. It was said because I meant it.

Let me begin with what might seem a banal point to add to a book on political strategy. One of the reasons that Philip was an inspiration is that he was very nice. I mean, always, whenever I met him. It wasn't a bland niceness. He was jumpy and intense and peppered you with questions. But it was a niceness entirely unaffected by coming from different political tribes. He didn't furrow his brow, perplexed that you could really believe such stupid things and ally yourself with such bad people. Nor was he secretly congratulating himself on a naughty liaison with the 'other side'. He was just interested and ready to listen, and to offer a bit, sometimes more than a bit, of himself.

This was attractive enough in itself, and an example I learned from. But it deserved the description 'inspirational' for a further reason. Philip Gould behaved like that because he was always learning from people.

During Philip Gould's career, politics changed fundamentally. Some of that was because of him, some he merely understood better than most people. And much of it had to do with the way politicians and political strategists began to understand voters better.

A year before the general election in 2009, Britons went to vote in the European elections. The result was catastrophic for Labour. Indeed, I described it, on the television results show I was appearing on, as 'a great result for Michael Foot'. This is because Gordon Brown's party had done so badly that it made Labour's 1983 election result seem like a triumph.

Yet to compare the modern Labour Party unfavourably with Michael Foot's, a grasp of mathematics is only one requirement. The other thing you need to have is a defective memory. It is not necessary to hold Gordon Brown's leadership in high regard to assert that between 1979 and 1983, Labour was immeasurably worse. It was ideologically split between people whose ideas were plainly mad and others who were merely completely wrong about almost everything.

The split produced a contest for the deputy leadership that dragged in all its main players. The most electorally attractive figures left the party altogether. The party's candidate for Prime Minister would have been a more credible candidate if he had been put forward for a minor literary prize. And its election manifesto was so obviously rambling, impractical and unpopular that a member of the Shadow Cabinet dubbed it 'the longest suicide note in history'.

The correct response, therefore, to hearing that Labour did worse than in 1983 is not just to say 'gosh'. It is to ask 'why?' And the answer is to be found in changes to the electorate.

In his book *Tides of Consent*, the American political scientist James Stimson argues that voters can be divided into three groups. The first group he calls 'the Passionate'. These are people 'who care a great deal about public affairs, have strong views, and form lasting commitments to one side or another'. In what is no more than a common-sense observation, Professor Stimson argues that these people don't settle elections. They can't because they don't move their vote and tend to interpret political events in a way conditioned by their existing view.

A second group he labels 'the Uninvolved'. These are 'people who think politics isn't important in their lives (and they are probably right), don't pay attention and don't want to be bothered'. The Uninvolved often don't vote, and what moves them politically hither and hither has a random character, with one movement cancelling out another.

Which leaves Stimson's third group – 'the Scorekeepers'. The Scorekeepers 'are non-ideological pragmatists who trust or distrust each side equally. They tend to see politics not as a contest of world views, but merely as alternate teams of possible managers of government, each contending that they can do a better job. The Scorekeepers are not choosing directions in their votes, they are hiring managers.'

It is this group – pragmatic, ready to change sides, involved enough to care – that really accounts for Professor Stimson's political tides.

What we have seen in the past 30 years is a shift from 'the Passionate' group, swelling the ranks of 'the Scorekeepers'. This changes politics in two ways. First, it makes elections more volatile. Votes are lent to parties, rather than given them for life. A party that wins a healthy majority in one election can lose by a landslide in the next. The base vote that was once prepared to turn out even for Michael Foot is much diminished.

The second change is that politics has become more pragmatic, less partisan, more inclined to a sort of cool centrist position. Politicians who seem obsessive or extreme are unattractive to the Scorekeepers. The ability of leaders to communicate, matters more as voters 'interview' their next Prime Minister before hiring him or her. The quality of the chief executive is more important than the party's identity. Try to fight an election with a leader even slightly inferior to the alternative on offer and you risk being slaughtered.

I think Philip Gould was among the first people in British politics to understand that this was happening and to try to fashion a response.

In British politics, people have long chosen their tribe along class lines. Labour could rely on working-class solidarity. Voting Conservative was part of the middle-class package. There was a big gulf between the two, and moving from one to the other seemed unthinkable for many people. It would have involved changing who they are. Membership of 'the Passionate' was a statement of identity, much more than of ideology.

In the suburbs where Philip learned his politics, he could see that class composition was changing, the middle class was growing and that while it saw Labour as alien, it could be detached from the Conservatives. These voters no longer saw being Tory as part of their identity.

His response was three-fold. The first was to find a candidate who could appeal to the Scorekeepers. Tony Blair was ideal. He understood the Scorekeepers completely because he was one. Labour was not part of his identity and his most characteristic political statement is 'what counts is what works'. To read his memoirs is to be struck by the extent to which he was a pragmatic centrist, detached from his party label.

I don't think Mr Blair would have been as successful without Philip. But, equally, it is worth noting that without him – or someone like him – Philip's politics couldn't work electorally. And didn't.

I remember Philip saying over lunch in the days just before Mr Blair left Downing Street that 'Gordon knows that he needs to change.' When he said those words I instantly realised that Mr Brown would be a disaster electorally, because people don't change. I also reflected that it was admirable but also noteworthy how loyal Philip was to his allies and to his party, since it was obvious that Mr Brown had at times treated him very roughly, and it was also clear that Philip intuited that Mr Brown's attempts to change would end in failure.

And I thought it deeply impressive that Philip could be so committed to his tribe, so obviously one of 'the Passionate' himself, yet so capable of understanding how Scorekeepers think and what was necessary to appeal to them. Most people in politics tend to equate their own view of the world with the electorally popular view. Philip never made that mistake.

The second part of Philip's response to the rise of the Scorekeepers was to treat every day as if were a referendum on Tony Blair and his leadership. If people were keeping score, he wanted to know what score they were keeping. And he did it through focus groups.

So-called 'focus group politics' are often attacked. But only by people who don't use focus groups, haven't attended one and fail to understand how they work. Philip was often criticised by those who thought he was practising voodoo magic, or others who felt he was advocating the abandonment of belief and principle in favour of chasing votes.

The first time I was involved with groups, I realised what nonsense this criticism was. After the 1997 election, Gordon Brown announced some extra spending on health and education. He gave very precise numbers, having rolled several years of spending into one. It had led the news for several days and I was keen to know what voters thought. I – then the director of the Conservative Research Department – eagerly awaited the results of the focus groups. We hadn't done many of them up to that point.

What came back, changed my outlook on politics. It turned out that the voters had never heard of Mr Brown's announcement. It sounded to them quite a good idea, although they were very sceptical that it would really happen, thinking it more likely to be a conjuring trick. They were also extremely hazy about the difference between millions and billions. The exact numbers, in other words, meant nothing to them. And if we hadn't brought it up, the whole thing would have passed them by entirely.

In the years that followed I was to encounter this sort of thing more and more. The group asked to name 'one other Conservative apart from David Cameron' ('Erm, Ed Miliband'; 'Oh, yes, that's right, and his brother Ed Balls'). The group asked to name 'any Jew in public life' ('Got it … Whoopi Goldberg'). And so on.

So the idea that focus groups could determine policy was ridiculous. Views were far too ill-formed and ill-informed to do that. If you asked a group how to run the NHS you wouldn't get a coherent answer. Even if you wanted to follow what the groups said, you couldn't.

The scientific critique – that it is voodoo – has more to it. Focus groups are hopeless as a formal tool of research. But they are nevertheless extraordinarily useful in understanding how people respond to issues and what is on their mind, at least when coupled with proper representative surveys. You learn how people understand what happens in politics and how they are experiencing what they do.

Those who argue that consulting focus groups leads to the wishy-washy politics of compromise and the lowest common denominator might, with profit, consider the issue of crime policy. In 1997, the sociologist James Q. Wilson wrote an essay in *The Public Interest* on crime rates in America and the United Kingdom. Why, he asked, had US crime rates been falling as UK crime rates rose? A large part of his answer was simply that US policy-makers had become more responsive to public opinion. Under pressure to address the problem, they had begun to develop creative solutions. And these solutions worked.

By contrast, deep into the 1990s it was acceptable in Britain for politicians to shrug their shoulder in the belief that crime rises were inevitable, that it was a tide that couldn't be turned back. The former Home Secretary Roy Jenkins, for instance, made this argument explicitly. He said that it was foolish for any politician to start talking about cutting crime.

Tony Blair made his reputation by realising that the public did not accept this. And that crime was a particular problem for those people who might vote Labour, or already voted Labour. The techniques used by Philip led to a competition between the parties to develop crime policies that worked.

Conducting focus groups is therefore democratic. It ensures that elites don't lose touch with voters. More prosaically, it is simply essential professionally. In the era of the Scorekeepers, the party that fails to conduct focus group research will be massively disadvantaged. Indeed, much more than just focus groups. The ability to assess people's thoughts and opinions is going to grow, along with an increasing scientific understanding of where those attitudes come from. Political parties are going to be in an arms race of research techniques.

The sheer scale of Philip's operation only became clear to me when I read his book, *The Unfinished Revolution*. It immediately became obvious that when Labour talked to voters it knew what it was talking about, and how they would respond. At Central Office we were mainly guessing. Unsurprisingly, this didn't work all that well. I don't think any major party will be arrogant enough to try that again. Or at least, if they do, the results will be predictably poor.

The use of focus group research will long be associated with Philip, and rightly so. But just as important to the political success he enjoyed was his understanding that responding to the Scorekeepers required living in the modern world. This third part of Philip's response sounds like by far the easiest bit of it. But it isn't.

The founding of the Labour Party involved bringing together three things – the organisational power of the unions, the progressive values of liberal Britain and the doctrine of democratic socialism. From the beginning there were contradictions between these aspects of Labour, as Edmund Dell brilliantly describes in *A Strange Eventful History*, his biography of democratic socialism.

The biggest problem was that democratic socialism was built on an error, an understandable one to have made, but an error just the same. The founders of the party believed that the world was a simple place, and that it would be possible to plan and control economic activity. This was never true. It was a misunderstanding that ought to be excused people who didn't travel much and hadn't access to the technology that allows rapid communications.

But the extent of that misunderstanding and its importance only grew as technology grew. And it became increasingly unreasonable to fail to realise it. By the 1960s Labour was desperately trying to control a world that not only couldn't be controlled, but obviously couldn't. The attempt to plan the economy gave a role to the trade unions in national life that they lost the moment that planning was abandoned. And at the same time, traditional crafts were being replaced, sending existing unions into decline.

By the time Philip became a serious player in Labour politics, then, two parts of the compact that had made the party were largely obsolete. Failing to accept this made Labour sound – what in fact, it had become – absurdly out of touch. They disliked the cars, televisions and aspirations of their own voters.

What Philip understood was that this didn't rob his progressive liberal values of meaning. Or of an audience. But Labour would have to be remade if it was going to be effective in advancing those values. It would have to accept trade union reform, the consumer economy, the fact that some people become wealthy and get paid more than others, and the fact that Labour wasn't trusted as a custodian of the modern economy. This became the project of the modernisers.

Conservative modernisers faced a similar sort of problem in the 1990s. Conservative ideas were shackled to a party that disapproved of the lifestyle of the people whose votes it was seeking. Changing the party's attitude to gay rights, an ethnically diverse society and working women has often been criticised as irrelevant or as 'politically correct' but it was, and remains, essential.

There was, then, plenty that Conservative modernisers could learn from Philip Gould. And we did. In fact, it is very possibly the case that if Philip Gould had not written and published *The Unfinished Revolution*, David Cameron would not have become Prime Minister.

When the first edition appeared in 1998, the Conservative leader William Hague sent a copy of it to every member of the Shadow

Cabinet, and in each he wrote the words 'know thine enemy'. But for a small group of us – already convinced that the party needed a deeper analysis of the reasons for its defeat – the lessons it taught were far more profound. We used it not to understand our 'enemy', but to understand ourselves.

And the understanding we reached helped to provide David Cameron with the analysis which years later was an essential part of his victorious campaign to win the Conservative leadership.

Perhaps that understanding could have been reached in another way. And perhaps David Cameron's personal qualities could have won him the leadership without that understanding (although I doubt that he would then have won the premiership). But in practice that is not how it happened. First there was Gould, then came comprehension, then came the victorious leadership campaign.

So should Philip have written his book? There is certainly a political case against it. But it wouldn't have been Philip to keep his thoughts to himself. And if he had, the rest of us would have been robbed of a historical account of real importance and of an invaluable contribution to political strategy.

Like the man who wrote it, an inspiration.

Philip Gould and the Art of Political Strategy

8

Peter Hyman

There are very few people in politics who understand political strategy. Philip Gould was one of them.

Modern politics spawns archetypes: spin doctors, policy wonks, political secretaries, pollsters. These political operatives have their niche and their client groups, but too often fail to understand the pressures, constraints or motivation of each other.

The spin doctor spends his waking hours on the phone to journalists, tickling up columnists, trailing speeches, pre-empting bad news. His foe is the political lobby, hostile papers, 24-hour media. Spin doctors thrive on pace, intrigue, unpredictability; the wink, the nudge. First editions hitting the news stands; a blog, a tweet creating news out of gossip.

For the policy wonk, a good spreadsheet is the equivalent to a newspaper first edition. A juicy factual morsel in an Institute of Fiscal Studies report sets the heart racing. A seminar filled with professorial jousting about social mobility, public-spending pie charts, or patterns of migration, make life worth living. Symbolic policies, while looked down upon as 'cheap', 'populist' or 'pandering', are nonetheless seen by the policy guru as their moment of glory: 'That was my hypothecated tax in the manifesto.' 'I was the first to use the term Sure Start in 1994.' 'Congestion charging came out of my visit to Sweden in 1987.' Policy advisers see nuance as clever, necessary, essential to a good policy. Spin doctors see it as unsellable, impossible to capture in a headline, a recipe for confusion, wilful misinterpretation, and even political meltdown.

Political secretaries are the fixers, the bruisers, the schmoozers. In league with the Whip's office, they use flattery and menace, hand in glove, to achieve their primary outcome: support for the leader.

Without the political strategist these worlds – media, policy, public, politics – would remain forever at loggerheads, uncomprehending. The policy wonk never confronting reality, the spin doctor rarely having substance to sell, the pollster always reacting to, rather than leading, public opinion.

The political strategist is that rarest of political breeds. A person who brings order to chaos, someone who straddles these competing demands. He knows policy matters, for without substance a political party is an empty shell. He is well aware of the force of the public if angered, dismissed or patronised. He knows too that the media hunts in packs, devours the weak, ridicules those without momentum and direction.

Before we get on to the excellent, it is worth remembering that there is such a thing as a mediocre political strategist. The strategist who slavishly follows every belch of public opinion; who is too close to the media baron. The mediocre political strategist sees surface not depth: 'They hate you Prime Minister because you are out of touch.' 'You'll win back votes if you pass another Crime Bill.' The mediocre strategist fails to understand patterns and stories; the messenger counts as much as the message. Too often peddling a single line, he becomes known for one point of view, and so, as circumstances change, is left stranded, clutching hold of the sand on a disappearing shoreline. There are strategists who, whatever the country, whatever the crisis, resort to the same formula: 'You've got to be more populist, talk about the many not the few – attack those who are privileged.' Others will do the opposite, whatever's happening their response is: 'Bring the nation together, show how you are for all the people, end the politics of division.' The mediocre strategist has wisdom that turns to dogma – 'You can't win an election if you promise to raise taxes', 'The electorate only respond to two things: greed or fear', 'Negative campaigning always beats positive campaigning.'

Mediocre political strategists are often excellent at hiding their lack of insight.

So what makes a great political strategist? The power to synthesise; the ability to see the future; a questing, relentless, search for patterns and meaning. He needs to be comfortable in the rarefied atmosphere of the policy seminar as well as the intimidating brawl of the political lobby. A political strategist weaves and meshes, analyses and distils, packages and dismantles. In Philip's own words 'strategy should never be static but always evolving'. The job of the strategist is to spot when the small, incremental changes accumulate into something more profound and fundamental. A political strategist must be forward thinking, never trapped parroting as Thatcher and Blair both did on occasions that 'there is no alternative'. There is *always* an alternative.

Philip Gould could do all these things. He understood the tide of events and the symbolic moments. He could read mood and identify change. He could distinguish the spasms of public opinion from the harbinger of future disaster.

The Power of the Conversation

Philip believed it was through conversation and dialogue and what, in his Hegelian moments, he called 'dialectic', that he arrived at the right place. For Philip conversation built meaning and relationships. He wanted to get to the heart of the matter. The conversation between adviser and Prime Minister had to be grounded in reality; the dialogue between Prime Minister and public to be grown up, deep, conversational, nuanced and in one of his favourite word – 'connecting'.

The word 'iteration' was made for Philip; refinement after refinement – getting closer and closer to the central point. He came into his own when advising on the leader's speech at the Labour Party annual conference. This speech is the most strategic of the year. It sets the tone, develops key messages, provides new policy, gives party members a script, and defines how the party wishes to attack its opponents. Most of all, it attempts to connect with the public. We would work on drafts of the speeches in a cramped hotel room and debate for hours the subtleties of each line. Then Philip would go away and produce a forensic and crystal-clear summary of what needed to happen next. He didn't pull his punches: 'The difficulty with the speech comes as usual from a lack of clarity', was one of his more arresting first lines to Prime Minister Tony Blair on one of the less good drafts. He went on in similar vein: 'The problem of the speech is that it started with a structure based on transition and journey but has gradually evolved into a speech where the sense of journey has disappeared. The consequence is that though the speech is much tighter and tougher it lacks momentum, dynamism and vision.'

At Number 10, as head of Tony Blair's Strategic Communications Unit, I would spend many hours on the phone to Philip talking through strategy. A conversation with Philip skipped all small talk and got immediately to the point that needed resolving. 'Where are the Tories vulnerable?' 'Why are we in the wrong place on crime?' 'How do we develop a new politics that engages the public?'

This conversation on political strategy with Philip took many twists and turns over 20 years but the key components remained the same. What follows are some of the themes of those conversations, some of the tools in the political strategist's armoury, a few of the layers that build up the coherence and success of a political party.

Project and Purpose

There is craft to political strategy; but also moral purpose and values. Great political strategists cannot apply their bag of tricks to any party at any time. They are committed to a cause. Philip Gould was committed to the Labour Party and to Labour leaders. He was intensely loyal to all Labour leaders, however flawed. He talked a lot about the 'project'. For him it meant the big argument, the central purpose. For the left it meant a coalition of support from middle to working class – a programme for government that blended economic success with social justice, and a politics that was open, forward looking, dynamic and changing. I came to believe that the project had three interlocking strands. The great projects, the great strategists and politicians combine all three: what the country wants, what the country needs, what we believe. Some politicians start with what the country needs. Tony Blair instinctively began in this place. That is why modernisation of Britain's institutions and infrastructure was perhaps his most consistent theme. Other politicians, Thatcher perhaps, Gordon Brown at his best, start from what they believe and try to impose that on the country. Others are more pragmatic – pandering even – starting from the public and trying to reflect what they want. As Figure 8.1 shows, the intersection of all three produces a winning formula. And for three elections Labour's belief in a strong economy with renewed public services won broad support. Iraq is a good example of what can go wrong when a policy fails to fit in any of these interlocking circles: not part of Labour values, not what the public wants, and difficult to convince people that

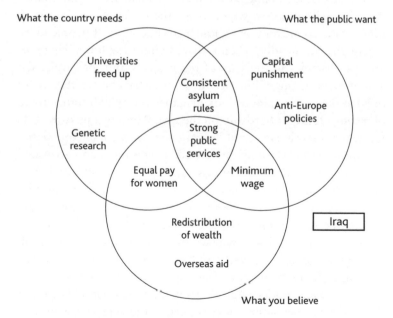

Figure 8.1 Interlocking strands of the project

it was what the country needed. The problem for today's Tories is that it is not clear what they believe, they are too often out of step with what the public wants, and they have failed to convince that the current economic medicine is what the country needs. That is why both their coalition in the country and coalition in government are both fragile.

Message

I spent more time talking to Philip about message than almost anything else. Message is explanation, compass, reassurance. It is the washing line that policy hangs off. Message turns mush into clarity, public anger into comprehension, impatience into understanding.

Message is multi-layered.

Narrative. We talk of narrative and that's where it starts. What is the journey we are taking the country on? What are the landmarks? And how will we know when we get there? A sense of journey is utterly vital to prevent being knocked off course. If people know where you are heading then setbacks count for little. There are always obstacles in the way of big projects and the public will accept them. If the public do not know what the sacrifice is for, or what the sunny uplands look like, then they will be unforgiving of incompetence or hardship on the way. Painting a picture of the future is not sentimental, indulgent or airy-fairy, but the foundation of a meaningful relationship between government and governed.

Definition. At the heart of this narrative are values or what we often called 'definition'. Who are we and what do we stand for? For Blair this was a given. However much we pleaded with him to spell out *why* we were doing things, he would retort 'Our values are not the problem. People know why we are doing things, they just doubt our competence to do them.' This had some truth in it. People were more flexible on the means of getting to their destination – 'what matters is what works'. But it missed the fundamental point that the world was becoming more ethical, not less. People wanted to know that brands, organisations, products, parties were not just competent but embodied the right instincts and values. Trust is an elusive but hard-won political commodity. Trust breaks down quickly if you are only selling yourself on competence; for everyone makes mistakes. Trust erodes more slowly if you have cemented a relationship with the public anchored in shared beliefs.

Yet, despite Blair's reservations, more time was spent in the early years discussing the precise formulation of our values than any other message debate. This was a decade-long struggle to find the heart of New Labour. Which one word summed us up? Were we fundamentally a party of *opportunity* for all – social mobility, hope, optimism, the future? On the other hand, wasn't Blair's contribution to Labour's thinking as shadow Home Secretary before 1997, to talk effectively about personal *responsibility* and try to reclaim it as a Labour idea? Wasn't Blair's insight in fact that we needed both o*pportunity and responsibility*, that the need for reciprocity – give as well as take – is in fact the key insight of our time? Unfortunately it wasn't as simple as that. In 1994, the work of Amitai Etzioni and others on communitarianism was gathering pace and seemed to exemplify Blair's message. Individuals only prosper in a strong community, they said. Community became the Blair word in Opposition. Put it all together and our message seemed to be: opportunity + responsibility = community. That was Clinton's successful formula. Ours too for a while. But that was not the end of the discussion. Two pieces of the values jigsaw remained unplaced: modernisation AND equality. Blair stood for modernisation, modernisation of the Labour Party and modernisation of the country: New Labour, New Britain. This defined his appeal. But modernisation is value-free. Right and left can both modernise. What makes modernisation a project of the left? The answer was equality. Or fairness, the word that New Labour preferred because it lacked the Socialist overtones. All should share in the fruits of modernisation. That is how Philip got to *A Future Fair for All*, a slogan used more than once for the Labour Party conference. In my view, it was not particularly catchy, but it incorporated the strands of future and fairness very well. Every Labour leader since 1992 has juggled with these words:

opportunity, responsibility, community, modernisation, future, fairness. In the words of one jaundiced political commentator, at political lobby one afternoon, in his tenth year of being 'spun' a new formulation of New Labour's values: 'Does the order of these words really matter?' All I can say is, we thought it did.

The big argument. In government we started talking about 'winning' the big argument at about the same time as we were 'losing' the daily battle with the media. Out of necessity we moved from an obsession with daily spin, winning every news cycle, rebutting every falsehood, complaining at every inaccuracy, to a more elevated (relaxed would be overdoing it) approach that said what mattered was winning the debate over time. This is a profound decision for all parties and one with no right answer. Should politicians with reputations to build and protect, with 24-hour media desperate to fill space, with internet gossip fuelling media feeding frenzies, spend their time on the trivia because it shapes public perceptions – or should they let all this wash over them and just care about whether they are doing the right thing in the long run? The truth is probably that you need to do both. The trouble for us was that media rebuttal had turned into a deeply-held sense that we were both belligerent and paranoid. Blair, though obviously keen to uphold his own personal reputation, preferred to operate at the level of big arguments and there were many big arguments that needed to be won: why monolithic public services needed to be broken up, why Britain needed to be full players in Europe, why we needed to go to war on Iraq.

Process messages. It's mid-term. Shit is hitting the fan on a daily basis: fuel crisis, Foot and Mouth, ministerial resignations, spin-doctor crises, political-donations rows; all of it obscuring 'delivery'. The public think we have done nothing. When Philip hands out his questionnaire to the focus group and asks them to list all the good things about the government, blank sheets of paper are returned: 'Can't think of anything.' 'Dunno'. They got a big landslide, what have they done with it? Why should we vote for them ever again? So we sit down with Philip and try to work out a process message that (a) shows humility – there is no point listing achievements if the public don't want to listen; (b) allows us to remind people of what we have done, and (c) gives us a forward-looking message that outlines the mouthwatering policies and achievements to come. The result was one of our most prosaic but informative lines: *A lot done, a lot to do.* It's ringing simplicity is disarming. Trust me, it took hours to craft. A lot done (Minimum Wage, New Deal, cut class sizes, lowest inflation and mortgage rates, more money for schools and hospitals), a lot to do (public services reform, bring peace to Northern Ireland). At best, soundbites can represent the presence of thought, not its absence, and as such perhaps it is time to rehabilitate them.

Were the hours we spent discussing message the worst sort of navel-gazing or in fact the crux of the whole project?

Reflecting on message since leaving politics, I am now more acutely aware of the gap between language and deeds, message and reality. Words too often speak louder than actions; message becoming a substitute for doing.

The Gould Memo

Not having a desk in Number 10, Philip spread his influence not just through dialogue but through the exocet of the Gould memo. Always blunt, precise in its prescription, the Gould memo, usually written following focus groups, was the starting point for many of our strategic discussions.

Focus groups provided Philip with his oxygen supply of new thoughts and ideas. I would go to many of these groups with him. 'My name is Philip,' he would start, immediately charming his audience. 'I do this round the world. Today I am here with you in glorious Watford. Exactly how exciting is Watford? You may have done something like this for beer or another product. Today we are asking your opinion on politics so say whatever you like. I have a wife and two children and I live in north London. Let's go round the circle introducing ourselves and saying also what papers we read.' Despite doing the groups for many years I was staggered by how rude Philip could be in cutting off particularly boring members of the public mid-sentence. 'Thank you love, we've heard enough.'

The Philip Gould summary note of focus groups was one of the great pleasures of working at Number 10. We knew it was absurd to extrapolate the national mood from seven people in Watford, eight people in Milton Keynes, or six people in Putney, but Philip's skill was to use feedback from that small number to make a case that chimed in with the wider mood. Focus groups were merely the cloak under which Philip would produce the dagger we needed at the heart of our sometimes sloppy strategic thinking.

Election Campaigns

The political strategist comes into his own during an election campaign. The politics, the policy, the spin doctors all have to fit in to the overall strategy. And Philip was a brilliant election strategist. Elections brought together all his skills and was when he was at his most powerful.

The campaign would start a year out; we would meet with Philip to discuss the war book. The war book was the term used in the Clinton campaign for the document that mapped our strengths and weaknesses of our side and our opponents'. The document used polling data, policy ideas, an analysis of our position to determine on what grounds we should fight the election. Was this a play-it-safe campaign or a high-risk campaign; was it to be presidential in feel or show off the full team? Was it to focus on the economy and build out, or on social issues? Was it to be aimed exclusively at Middle England or try to get our traditional support to come out to vote? Was it to be among the people, town hall meetings, interactive or less risky and more staged performances? What were the symbolic policies or pledges?

At the heart of this war book were dividing lines; the contrast between the two parties. Many (Labour) versus the few (Tories), modernise the NHS (Labour) versus privatise the NHS (Tories), Investment in public services (Labour) versus cuts (Tories). This reached its height with the unexciting election slogan of 'Forward not back'.

What certainly worked was the way these dividing lines shaped the activity and speeches of an election campaign. All candidates could be in no doubt where they needed to position themselves.

Gordon Brown increasingly liked this approach to politics – it was tribal, black and white: Labour stands for this, Tories stand for that. Tony Blair could see its benefit during a campaign but instinctively believed that sticking too rigidly to political dividing lines constrained policy formation. Good policy, in his view, often broke through left and right boundaries and therefore made crude sloganising harder.

Philip enjoyed meshing all aspects of the election campaign: the party election broadcasts, the billboard advertising, the prime ministerial visits, the key messages, the forensic dismantling of opponents' policies, the last five days get-out-the-vote strategy. Where Philip showed genius was in understanding where the public was as election day approached. What was it that would push our supporters over the line? What message would hold back voters from switching sides? Just as ice cream makers never reveal their magic ingredients, Philip had a sixth sense of how all the flows of opinion were coalescing. Arguably his greatest achievement was to have prevented an overall Tory majority at the 2010 election when everything was stacked against Labour. In comparison, the three Blair victories, while hard won, were easier to achieve.

Twentieth-Century versus Twenty-First-Century Political Strategy

Philip started thinking about *new politics* before anyone else in the New Labour team. It was not just a response to the party being crucified by the press over 'spin'. Hundreds of focus groups over many years showed a growing distance between politics and the public. Philip encapsulated this in his concept of 'the Empty Stadium'. Politicians, he believed, were on the pitch kicking lumps out of each other, throwing everything they'd got into thrashing their opponents, but the public had gone home. They'd stopped watching; switched off. It was a ferocious game and those on the pitch enjoyed what they were doing. But it had failed to excite, entertain or enthrall anyone. The truth, if anything, was even worse. It was not so much an Empty Stadium as a stadium filled with a few very partisan supporters who tried to convince the players that the game had a point and obscured the fact that more normal, less obsessive supporters, had lost interest. In response, Philip developed a view of a participatory democracy. In practice, it was difficult to deliver. Yes, it could mean town hall meetings, initiatives like the 'Big Conversation' opening up policy-making to all-comers. But in reality there was a limit to how much politicians genuinely wanted the public to express their views.

Increasingly, with huge developments in Web 2.0 technology, participation has become easier. But even with blogging, YouTube, and every MP tweeting, it is the big media players and politicians who still dominate and the voice of the people is still often unheard. I debated at length with Philip my view that politics was becoming both more local and more global, with the middle tier – national politics – becoming hollowed out. At the local level there is energy, often dynamism, in social entrepreneurs, voluntary organisations, trying to make things happen. Globally, while the institutions are often not fit for purpose, there are issues of huge significance being shaped by powers and companies. But at the national level there is a stale battle between politicians and the media, that has now culminated in the phone-hacking scandals. But well before these surfaced, the relationship between politicians and the media needed a new settlement so that complexity and real debate had a chance of succeeding.

Philip understood that the world had changed dramatically since 1997 and that the old certainties of political strategy would not work. Renewal in politics is always hard. Consistency is prized over adaptability. It's hard to say openly, 'My thinking has moved on.' Renewal is particularly hard in office. The group of politicians who created New Labour were formed and scarred by Labour's disasters in the 1980s. They were determined to do and say the opposite to everything that had gone before, particularly anything associated with the 1983 'longest suicide note in history' manifesto. This meant that they were at times locked into positions that were as dogmatic in the opposite direction as the policies they opposed so vehemently. The result was that however much circumstances changed, they found it hard to move beyond a zealous pro-Europeanism to replace 1983 withdrawal from Europe, advocacy of no tax rises to replace the 'pips squeaking' in the 1970s and 1980s, no inch given on defence in reaction to unilateralism, antagonism or indifference to green issues for fear they would seem wacky, a cosy relationship with the press as a reaction to the *Sun* destroying Neil Kinnock, and a sycophancy towards business so as 'never again would Labour enter an election with no businesses on their side'. This made renewal very hard indeed. Philip, possibly because he was not a politician and had few previous utterances on public record, could re-evaluate and move on. Where all of them, however, were right and have been vindicated is that New Labour brought, above all else, a hard-headedness to Labour politics, a willingness to confront reality and make tough decisions. Without this impetus from the top, Labour all too easily gets used to Opposition as a place where it can indulge in debate at the expense of action.

Philip's great achievement was to be both the premier proponent of twentieth-century campaigning techniques and to pioneer a new way of doing strategy for the twenty-first century.

Before 1997, Philip was an advocate of the craft learned from Clinton and others that the way back for the left was: (a) massive reassurance, (b) mainstream policies, and (c) war rooms and instant rebuttal. For parties of the left, consistency and being 'on message' was the antidote to the self-indulgent shambles of everyone saying their own thing. Instant rebuttal reflected the understandable recognition that most of the media was hostile and lies that go unchallenged stick around and get repeated. Philip was as good as anyone at the twentieth-century political game.

But ten years later he started to pioneer a political strategy more in tune with the twenty-first century: less rebuttal; more authentic, more participatory, winning arguments (Table 8.1).

Table 8.1   The changing landscape of the political strategist

Twentieth-century political strategy	Twenty-first-century political strategy
Centralised top-down democracy	Participatory democracy
Win the Westminster media game	Speak directly to the public
Consistency of message	Grown-up debate admitting error and doubts
Uniformity	Authenticity
Winning the 24-hour media cycle (tactics first)	Winning the big argument (strategy first)
Media relations are key	The 'project' is key

The Nature of Political Leadership

Philip understood that just as political strategy was evolving, so was the nature of leadership.

Possessing charisma himself, Philip liked to see it in political leaders. He had a deep understanding that modern politicians needed to be performers, show empathy and a connection with the public, but also have values, purpose and direction. He was not one of those pollsters or strategists who wanted the candidate to be packaged, identikit, fit some crude model of what a leader might look like. But he did want his Labour leaders to dominate a room. He didn't want to come out of meetings, as he often did, muttering at the lack of grip or steel.

One of the ongoing themes of our conversations was the balance between leading and listening. We were all conflicted on this, and Philip particularly so. Every fibre of his being told him that leaders had to be strong, yet his umbilical cord to the British people via focus groups and polling data suggested that listening, adapting, connecting would bring rich rewards.

Gouldism: Radical Labour

Philip was more than a great campaigner or pollster. He genuinely believed in a project. A project rooted in values that honoured and supported the struggle of ordinary families. He believed in the romance of politics, that without a cause politics becomes the pursuit of power for its own sake. Philip could renew. In 2012 he was thinking in a very different way from 1997. He was one of the few founders of New Labour, capable of genuine renewal. He believed in the idea of permanent revolution, a new dialectic, certainties and flows of opinion constantly being made and remade. It made him genuinely excited and restless to find a new path for the left. Political strategists don't have isms named after them. But Philip's brand of Labour politics, Gouldism if you like, genuinely attempted to combine global and local, public and private, liberal and egalitarian strands, leadership and listening, entrepreneurialism and solidarity, values and pragmatism. It is a view of the world, and how politics should be conducted, that might indeed prove longer lasting than New Labour.

His legacy is that at a time when Westminster politics is in danger of becoming stultifying, predictable, stale and out of touch, Philip was someone who could see how it need not be like that.

On a personal note, every single conversation I had with Philip left me with more ideas, more clues, more inspiration, more insight than at the start of the dialogue. I learnt more from him than any other person in my professional life. In anything I do in the future I will have Philip in my ear reminding me to think big, to believe, to look to the future, and to do the right thing.

How Philip Gould Helped to Save the Conservative Party

9

Andrew Cooper

New Labour, it turned out, did not mean 'New Danger'; the Conservatives were completely wrong about that.

The slogan and the argument it represented (and the infamous 'demon eyes' that became its visual motif) came, in the summer of 1996, as the end-point of months of internal Tory debate about what the right critique was of Tony Blair. Numerous different strategies against Labour were considered, based on an array of alternative assumptions about the palpably modernised party that lay before us. The Conservative leadership committed to an advertising campaign, but in truth never really settled on a consistent strategy and by the final, desperate, days the Tory attacks were random and sometimes contradictory. Among all the various theories about Tony Blair, the only one that seemed never occur to anyone was that Tony Blair might actually mean – and be, politically – what he said: that Labour modernisation was substantive and real. This thought didn't really cross my mind either until Philip Gould's book *The Unfinished Revolution* appeared in October 1998.

I can pinpoint precisely the first time I ever heard of Philip Gould: 12 September 1995, when a version of one of his long strategy notes to Tony Blair was leaked to the *Guardian*. Conservative Central Office reacted with predictable glee to the candour of the note and, in particular, its conclusion that 'Labour is not ready for government'. The press pored over the detail of the further reforms that Philip's leaked memo advocated, but there was little if any comment about the immensely telling fact that it had been written at all; the brutal frankness, the thoroughness and the intellectual rigour were all remarkable; nothing like that degree of perspective, clarity or ambition was in evidence within the Conservative Party. Amid the fleeting embarrassment of the leak for Labour, the significance of the document was largely missed. In the month before Philip Gould wrote his memo the Labour Party had an average opinion poll lead of 30 per cent, yet his analysis was as restlessly dissatisfied and as politically challenging as if they had trailed by the same huge margin. This was a man who had seen false dawns before, who had the most profound realisation of what it was that had made Labour unelectable and who was determined to leave nothing to chance.

It was more than three years later that the first edition of *The Unfinished Revolution* was published, an interlude during which I had moved from being head of research at a think tank to being in charge of private polling for the Conservative Party and then, in the shell-shocked months after the party's crushing ejection from power, its director of strategy.

It is – to state the blindingly obvious – incredibly difficult for politicians who have almost invariably believed in the efficacy and sense of the decisions they took in government to come to terms with rejection by the electorate, especially when it is as wholehearted, widely anticipated and warmly welcomed as the Conservative defeat in 1997. Many found the loss even harder to fathom because of the orthodox Tory view of New Labour.

Conventional Conservative wisdom held that after finding its own cherished convictions serially unpalatable to the voters, Labour only made itself electable by *pretending* to accept longstanding Conservative arguments on some key issues and adopting Tory positions wholesale on other issues, most importantly tax rates and public spending plans. This was of course diametrically opposite to the pre-election line that New Labour meant New Danger, but was nevertheless a view held much more widely and with much greater conviction – and no one really noticed or cared about the contradiction. But in the logic of the argument lay a strategic trap; or perhaps it was that the argument was a rationalisation of the reluctance to face difficult and unpalatable truths. For if it were true that Labour had only won by accepting Conservative arguments on many key issues, then by definition we Tories had no great need for regret, recrimination or change – or even much reflection about why we lost.

In those early months after the 1997 election the view of most Conservatives seemed to be that all we had to do was wait for the voters 'to come to their senses' about Labour. The only notable call for change came from Michael Portillo. Reinvented almost instantaneously by the manner of his own defeat, Portillo had been invited before the election to deliver a lecture at the autumn party conference fringe meeting of the Centre for Policy Studies think tank, the self-regarding keeper of the flame of Thatcherism. The speech received little media coverage; most journalists were interested in it only as the source of possible stories about 'Tory splits'. Portillo started by listing what he saw as the four principal factors behind the Conservative defeat. 'We must', he said, 'face these issues head on and deal with them':

First, the party became associated increasingly with the most disagreeable messages and thoughts ... Tories were linked to harshness: thought to be uncaring about unemployment, poverty, poor housing, disability and single parenthood; considered indifferent to the moral arguments over landmines and arm sales. We were thought to favour greed and the unqualified pursuit of the free market, with a 'devil take the hindmost' attitude.

Second, we abandoned almost completely the qualities of loyalty and the bonds of party without which a party effectively ceases to exist.

Thirdly, we were thought to be arrogant and out of touch ... Some of it was insensitivity – using the language of economics and high finance when people's jobs and self-esteem were at stake. And when people looked at the composition of our party, they thought it too elderly or too vulgar or too out of touch in vocabulary and perceptions, or in other ways unfamiliar and unrepresentative.

Fourth, there was sleaze ... which disgraced us in the eyes of the public. Their perception was of corruption and unfitness for public service. Such distasteful perceptions can endure and do us damage for a long time.

The speech went on to stress, in what is perhaps the simplest reduction of the modernisers' creed, that 'it is extremely important for the Conservative Party to deal with the world as it is now' and to show that it 'comprehends the diversity of human nature'.

It was a brilliant, honest analysis that could and should have fired up the modernising movement in the Conservative Party. But it didn't. It was launched into a vacuum and prompted no political reaction at all. The thoughts died in the airless atmosphere of denial that pervaded the Conservative Party. A year later – after 18 months in Opposition – the Tories had still made virtually no progress at all. Voting polls had us languishing in the mid-twenties. In focus groups former Conservative voters saw the party as no more electable than they had in May 1997.

It wasn't that we had done nothing in that year and a half. A wide-ranging process of institutional reform had, among other things, introduced 'one member, one vote' for leadership elections and created an Ethics & Integrity Committee to deal with future outbreaks of the sleaze that had been a recurring theme of John Major's government. Conservative Central Office in Smith Square (later to become, with exquisite irony, the UK base of the European Commission) – an old-fashioned and impractical warren of small offices and inefficient spaces – was physically reconfigured so we could establish an integrated 'War Room' along the lines pioneered by (or at least generally attributed to) Bill Clinton's 1992 presidential campaign. The business turnaround genius Archie Norman, newly elected as a Tory MP, became the party's Chief Executive, exerting an almost immediate inspirational, revitalising impact on the senior staff and, in a matter of months, heaving the whole culture of the building into the modern world. Structurally the party had modernised; but politically it hadn't.

As the party's strategy director from the summer of 1998, I spent much of my time digesting focus group and opinion poll evidence of how people viewed us. It was unremittingly bleak – all the more so because by the autumn of 1998 the Labour government's honeymoon was over and the mood of disappointed expectation was tangible. It didn't feel, to most voters, like the new dawn that Tony Blair had promised. But the Conservative Party was gaining no traction at all. To all but the Tory true-believers, we were unthinkable. Eighteen months on from the election, focus groups even of former Conservative voters were summing up the Tories as 'stagnant', 'irrelevant', 'selfish', 'old-fashioned', 'out of date' and even 'dead'. Private polling reported a remorselessly negative picture of how we were perceived. More than two-thirds of the electorate thought we weren't listening and were uncaring, disunited and out of touch. Three-quarters of voters rejected the proposition that 'the Conservative Party has changed for the better since the election' – and the only people who did think this was true were die-hard Tory supporters, many of whom didn't even want us to change. Even as the feeling grew that Tony Blair's government was not delivering the changes people had hoped for, Labour's poll lead over the Conservatives on key issues was widening, not narrowing. At the end of 1998 our polling showed us trailing by 14 per cent on law and order, by 25 per cent on the economy, by 40 per cent on education and by 43 per cent on the NHS, which voters ranked as the most important issue of all.

It was blindingly obvious that we desperately needed a new strategy; it was equally obvious that most Conservatives didn't recognise this need. That was where we were when Philip Gould's book *The Unfinished Revolution* landed on my desk in October 1998.

It was not written in the standard, desiccated style of most books about political campaigning. It was a handbook on political strategy told as a human story. The origin of Philip's modernising passion lay in his own life and the people around whom he'd grown up; people who he believed *should* be Labour voters but were not. He understood and articulated two vital truths: that the things putting people off the Labour Party were real and substantial, not presentational or marginal; and that Labour had betrayed these voters, not the other way around. The old, one-dimensional, class-based orthodoxy in the Labour Party held, in effect, that poorer people and those reliant on benefits, working in blue-collar jobs or living in council houses owed Labour an obligation of support. But, as Philip starkly noted in the introduction to *The Unfinished Revolution*,

> Labour had failed to understand that the old working class was becoming a new middle class: aspiring, consuming, choosing what was best for themselves and their families. They had outgrown crude collectivism and left it behind in the supermarket car park. I knew this because they were my life.

Philip saw with brilliant clarity that the progress of economic, social and cultural change had made political allegiance, which was fairly static in earlier generations, increasingly dynamic. Labour had disapproved of council house sales because the old fault-lines of politics meant that when someone became a home-owner they were crossing a political divide – in economic terms, from labour to capital. If you rented your home from the council, you voted Labour; if you had the means and the desire to buy your home, you probably didn't. The absence of aspiration was hard-wired into the traditional Labour view of its natural voter base. For Philip, *The Unfinished Revolution* was:

> The post-war journey of the hard-working majority as they moved from austerity to aspiration and demanded a new politics to match their new ambition ... and the parallel journey of the Labour Party as it moved, over almost a century, from representing the people, to ignoring the people, to betraying the people, until finally it became the people's party again.

This critique was the foundational insight of New Labour; the point Tony Blair was making when he said at the 1996 Labour conference:

> I can vividly recall the exact moment that I knew the last election was lost. I was canvassing in the Midlands on an ordinary suburban estate. I met a man polishing his Ford Sierra, self-employed electrician, Dad always voted Labour. He used to vote Labour, he said, but he bought his own home, he had set up his own business, he was doing quite nicely, so he said 'I've become a Tory'. He was not rich but he was doing better than he did, and as far as he was concerned, being better off meant being Tory too.

Margaret Thatcher had, in fact, made essentially the same point when, in the very first sentence of her introduction to the 1979 Conservative Party manifesto, she wrote 'For me the heart of politics is not political theory, it is people and how they want to live their lives.' How people wanted to live their lives now included owning their homes, having decent cars, buying nice things, going on foreign holidays, accumulating wealth and passing it onto their children. Wanting this should not be, Philip argued, incompatible with Labour values; and the perception that it was, is why Labour could not win in 1983 or 1987 or 1992 – and wouldn't win again until progressive values allowed for these goods and chattels of aspiration.

One of the most striking insights for Tory modernisation from *The Unfinished Revolution* was this unflinching intellectual clarity about why the party had lost. It was unarguable that we had not held ourselves to the same standard. In his introduction to the second edition of *The Unfinished Revolution*, published in September 2011, Tony Blair identifies this as one of the book's most important lessons: 'start with an honest analysis of why you are in opposition, not in government'.

This is harder than it sounds. The Labour Party has certainly not conducted an honest analysis of why it is in Opposition now; that is why it has failed to put forward a serious alternative argument about how to deal with the country's debt crisis and how it contrived to oppose government welfare reforms that go to the heart of why so many people had come to the view by 2010 that it was time for a change from Labour. The Conservative Party resisted for nearly a decade facing up to the reasons why it was in Opposition after 1997.

It is much easier to look only forward and politicians readily persuade themselves that to dwell on the causes of defeat is self-indulgent introspection. And – obviously – not everyone will agree on the honest analysis.

William Hague bravely confronted the Conservative Party with the reasons for its 1997 defeat in his very first party conference leader's speech. 'I know why we lost,' he said, 'and I think you do too. People thought we had lost touch with those we claimed to represent. Our Parliamentary party came to be seen as divided, arrogant, selfish and conceited. Our party as a whole was regarded as out of touch and irrelevant ... so we need to change our attitudes, change our organisation, change our culture.'

Philip Gould's approach went even further. It wasn't enough just to accept how the party had come to be *seen*; we needed to be brutally honest with ourselves about how much of this perception was *true*. Most senior Conservatives were arguing that the voters' damning judgement of our character, values and culture was a misconception spawned by a biased media, a slick Labour spin machine and one or two bad Tory eggs. This was profoundly complacent and strategically disastrous. If we were not able to see that at least some of what voters thought of us was real, we would be, in effect, denying the election result - telling the electorate they were wrong.

But the Tory party did not yet want to hear it. Within a few months of the 1997 election the most common mantra of Conservative MPs and activists had become 'we've apologised enough', an assertion which was neither true – since the voters hadn't noticed us apologising at all – nor remotely relevant, since the need was not to apologise, but to see ourselves from the electorate's point of view and properly to understand why they so fervently wanted rid of us.

There was simply no appetite for debating why we were in Opposition not government, let alone for considering the need for the Conservative Party to change. I was reminded of the comment by Clinton strategist Dick Morris in the wake of the disastrous congressional election defeat for the Democrats in 1994: 'They behaved as if their defeat had been a mere typographical error. It was if they were waiting for a recount to restore their mandate. The strategy seemed foolish to me. The electorate had spoken. To ignore this was suicidal.'

The Unfinished Revolution spurred me to push harder for modernisation. I was already working on a long strategy proposal and I now went back to it and hardened the analysis. Presented to the party leadership in November 1998, the *Kitchen Table Conservatives* paper asserted that:

> Recovery cannot begin until we recognise that a lot of the things people said about us before the election were true. That is why the perceptions have been hard to shift. We *were* out of touch. We *had* stopped listening. We *were* undisciplined and divided. We *didn't* have any clear idea of the direction in which we wanted to take Britain.

The *Kitchen Table* paper, as it was known, asserted that the Tory defeat had been even worse than generally supposed, citing detailed poll data showing the 'churn' of voters between the 1992 election – when the Conservatives had garnered what remains the largest popular vote in British history – and 1997, when they had won their lowest vote share since universal suffrage. The comfortable theory in right-wing Tory circles was that most of the voters the party lost in 1997 had just stayed at home, rather than switched to other parties; they were still Conservatives at heart, this view maintained, and would return to the fold once the Tory party returned to full-strength Thatcherism.

This arrogant presumption was the direct Tory equivalent of the hubristic Old Labour complacency that working-class voters should always vote Labour, and betrayed the same total misunderstanding about how most voters think about politics. Challenging the fallacy was as important in the Conservative recovery as it had been in the creation of New Labour.

As Tony Blair observed in his brilliant memoir *A Journey*:

> The single hardest thing for a practising politician to understand is that most people, most of the time, don't give politics a first thought all day long. Or if they do it is with a sigh, or a harrumph or a raising of the eyebrows, before they go back to worrying about the kids, the parents, the mortgage, the boss, their friends, their weight, their health, sex and rock n' roll ... For most normal people politics is a distant, occasionally irritating fog.

The failure of most politicians to comprehend this simple fact about the people they aspire to govern is, in Blair's words, 'a fatal flaw in most politicians'; fatal because 'it leads them to focus on the small not the big picture ... it stops them from understanding what really moves and matters'.

For most politicians their political identification is a very important component of their personal identity – often the most important piece of all. For most non-politicians political identification isn't important at all; it isn't something they even think about. The great majority are not adherents. Pollsters sometimes ask people which party they most identify with and, as is the way with poll questions, many will offer an answer. But it is rarely a strongly-felt affiliation. Most voters just aren't that interested.

The big picture of the 1997 election was that the Conservatives got 4.5 million fewer votes than they had five years earlier. Just under a million people who'd voted Tory in 1992 did stay at home in 1997. About three-quarters of a million voted for the Referendum Party or UKIP. But nearly 1.5 million former Tory voters had switched to the Liberal Democrats and over 2.2 million had gone directly to Labour.

Five years later we did some detailed qualitative research among some of those voters who had backed the Conservatives in 1992 and 1987 (and, if they were old enough, 1983) but then voted Labour in 1997. They weren't sorry in the least. They didn't feel remotely like thwarted Conservatives or reluctant Labour. They saw themselves simply as people who had voted Conservative for a period, when the Tories seemed to represent their values and understand their priorities, and now voted Labour because Tony Blair was much more in tune with what they wanted and were concerned about. That is how most people decide how to vote; people and how they want to live their lives.

The *Kitchen Table* paper filled a void and – mainly just for that reason – gained traction internally for a few weeks, but it quickly became clear that very few really agreed with the analysis and no one was following the strategic path it outlined.

Among a number of direct quotes from *The Unfinished Revolution*, the paper referred to one of the great Gould innovations: qualitative goals. Parties always have quantitative goals; Philip described how Labour had set a range of progress targets during the 1987–92 Parliament: to establish a poll lead, to be winning by-elections, to make net gains in the European elections, to makes inroads into Tory seats at council elections. Neil Kinnock's Labour Party met all of its quantitative goals. As a result conventional wisdom suggested he was firmly on course for victory. But Philip Gould's measure of progress was subtler and more guttural. He had defined four attitudinal goals. If they were capable of winning, the reactions of swing voters in Philip's focus groups needed to reflect four key thoughts about Labour: 'Labour has changed. Neil Kinnock has delivered a new Labour Party'; 'I trust Labour to form a government'; 'Labour has sensible economic policies and the team to run them'; 'Labour understands people like me'. However much the polls pointed to Labour victory, these attitudinal goals were never met – and Philip knew that Labour wouldn't win.

We translated this approach directly into some broad attitudinal goals of our own. Firstly, we needed voters to believe that 'the Conservative Party is really changing'. Secondly, over time, we needed more and more agreement that 'the Conservative Party knows what people really care about, says what people really think and has policies to deal with the things that really matter'.

Kitchen Table Conservatives advocated a change of tone, agenda and language. It urged some '10,000 volt initiatives' – another concept lifted from Philip Gould, who had written of the need for what he called 'electric shocks' to provide tangible, high news-value proof of change. The paper ended with a seven-point checklist of changes we needed to make:

- Speaking about the issues people really care about: kitchen table issues, not Westminster issues.
- Being prepared to change our agenda, *not* just continuing on auto-pilot.

- Using opinion polling – and really listening – to understand what people care about, *not* relying on guesswork.
- Being positive and having ideas, *not* just attacking Labour.
- Being prepared to take risks and controversial stands, *not* being too cautious.
- Realising that we have to change the way that we look and sound, *not* just carry on as we are.
- Ruthless organisation and purpose, *not* banking on Labour becoming unpopular.

Looking back at the list it seems unambitious and there are some big omissions. But it was a start. And it was going much too far for most Tories at the time. We weren't putting a modernising strategy into effect because most just didn't agree with it. And efforts to disseminate the ideas in the *Kitchen Table* paper through a series of briefing meetings for Tory MPs backfired badly. On 1 February 1999 *The Times* splashed with the headline 'Hague told to ignore "focus group fascism"', reporting that 'leading Tories accuse Central Office of becoming obsessed with the campaigning techniques that helped Labour to power'.

I wrote a second strategy paper, attempting to address the barriers that had meant no-one had followed the first one. This paper started with another headline from *The Times*. The paper had reported its January MORI poll (Labour 56 per cent, Conservatives 24 per cent, Lib Dems 14 per cent) beneath the heading 'People worry about hospitals, fear for their jobs and hate sleaze – but they still love Labour'. The description of voter grumbles was right, but the conclusion was wrong. They didn't still love Labour. Our private research found mounting (and, in truth, unreasonable) frustration that Tony Blair's government 'promise a lot but don't seem to do anything'. Labour in 1999 would still have passed Philip's attitudinal goals from 1989, but Labour in government didn't feel anything like as different as many voters had hoped. The fact that they had an even bigger lead than at the general election was not because people still loved Labour; it was, as I asserted in my strategy note, because 'they still loathe

the Conservatives. Labour's opinion poll rating is propped up by our failure to change the Conservative Party.'

The paper was called *Conceding and Moving On*. Both the phrase and the insight came from *The Unfinished Revolution*. Philip saw that Labour had, in the late 1980s and early 1990s, got itself stuck intellectually and politically – had become, as Kinnock put it in 1987, quoting Bevan, 'symbol worshippers'. In order to move on, Philip argued, Labour simply had to concede that on some issues they had lost the argument: 'on privatisation, on crime, on markets, the issue was settled'. 'Conceding and moving on' is the single hardest aspect of modernisation; it took Labour well over a decade and most Conservatives longer.

My paper argued that the central point holding us back in early 1999 and which we had to concede was 'however bad the Labour government turns out to be and however let down the British people feel, they will never, ever, regret getting rid of the last Conservative government'. We said the Conservative Party was changing, but the impulse to defend every dot and comma of the Major government proved that it wasn't. The readiness with which leading Conservatives allowed themselves to be lured by Labour into refighting the arguments of the 1992–97 Parliament showed how far we were from an honest analysis of why we were in Opposition, not in government. As the *Conceding and Moving On* paper noted, 'no matter how badly Labour is doing and how ever many times we run the arguments of the 1997 election by proxy, they will always win and we will always lose'. The two contrasts that worked for Tony Blair were those between New Labour and Old Labour and between New Labour and the old Tory government. The contrast we had to get to was between tarnished New Labour and a changed Conservative Party.

Everyone hated the *Conceding and Moving On* paper, apart from a cell of convinced modernisers scattered among the party's senior staff and a handful, at most, of Tory MPs. Most Conservatives just didn't want to concede – more to the point, didn't think they had anything *to* concede – and didn't accept that concession was needed in order to move on. Many also took exception to such a direct a lift from the New Labour playbook and the fact that I had even used (and attributed to him) Philip Gould's phrase.

Operationally we tried to get the party staff into more of a modernising mindset. Sheets went up on the walls in the HQ War Room – a sort of crib-sheet for *Kitchen Table Conservatives*:

1. Concentrate on the issues that really matter to people.
2. Use the language of people, not of politicians.
3. Show – as well as say – that we're listening.
4. Talk about the future, not about the past.
5. Concede and move on.
6. Be for things and people, not against things and people.
7. Have a sense of proportion.
8. Show integrity: be consistent, honest and likeable.

It was unarguably clear, however, by the spring of 1999, that modernisation had no momentum in the Conservative Party. I left my job as strategy director in circumstances that in the football world would be described as 'by mutual consent'.

Through the rest of that Parliament and all of the next, the Conservatives made virtually no progress. Apart from the occasional blip here and there – including a brief period in September 2000 when a fuel strike resulted in the first Conservative poll lead since early 1993 – and while the popularity of Tony Blair and his government eked away, Tory support barely flickered above its flatline: 31 per cent of the vote at the 1997 election became 32 per cent in 2001 and 33 per cent in 2005; it was the political equivalent of the 'dead cat bounce'.

In fact the situation was worse than that. The Tories were often said to be pursuing a 'core vote' strategy, but the true Conservative core had always been, in the parlance of political science, 'ABC1 voters': the professional, managerial and clerical classes. The bedrock of Margaret Thatcher's election victories had been leads over Labour of 35–40 per cent among these voters. Even in 1992 – a somewhat closer election – the Conservatives beat Labour by more than 30 per cent among ABC1s. This margin collapsed to just 5 per cent in 1997 – and fell again in 2001 and again in 2005, when the Conservative Party led Labour among this group by just 1 per cent.

In 1992 50 per cent of C1s – the socio-economic group that broadly comprises the aspirational middle classes – voted Tory. In 2005 only 32 per cent did so. The extra 1 per cent the Conservatives gained in 2001 and 2005 came from blue-collar voters. Margaret Thatcher's three election victories famously won crossover votes from working-class people, but did so while maintaining a massive lead among the middle-class Tory core. The pendulum wasn't swinging back; in 2001 and 2005, the election campaign it took to win a small gain for the Tories among manual workers repelled an almost equal number of middle-class people, especially women.

The push for modernisation had flickered briefly. At the 2002 party conference, then party Chair Theresa May provoked heckling when she told the Tory faithful that 'Our base is too narrow and so, occasionally, are our sympathies. You know what some people call us: the nasty party.' It was a depressing sign of how deeply most Conservative activists were still in denial; they weren't even willing to be told how the party was *perceived*, let alone to consider that it might actually need to change in order to challenge these perceptions.

At the subsequent election, after eight years in Opposition, more than half of voters still judged the Conservatives to be 'stuck in the past' and 'not interested in the problems of ordinary people'. Nearly half thought the Tories were 'narrow-minded and bigoted' and less than a third that the Conservative Party 'shares my values'. An ICM poll in February 2005 famously found that net agreement with a summary of Conservative policy on immigration fell by 30 per cent when voters were informed which party's policy it was. It was a damning indictment of how the party's motives and character were perceived. The unchanged, unmodernised Conservative Party duly suffered its third consecutive defeat three months later.

By then Philip Gould and I had become good friends. I met him at *The Times* newspaper's evening reception at the Labour Party conference in 2003. As the paper's pollster I attended all the annual conferences, presenting to a fringe meeting audience detailed poll findings on how their party was viewed by the voters. Though he felt a deep tribal bond with the Labour Party, Philip, unlike many others, had no awkwardness about discussing public opinion and political strategy with someone from the other side. He was a total loyalist without a whiff of sectarianism.

My immediate impression was of immense personal warmth, a restless mind and an exuberant spirit. Like Gatsby, he had an extraordinary gift for hope. Philip Gould was also, I soon discovered, a man of great intellectual generosity, always ready to share his insights and to debate the subtle nuances of public opinion and political strategy – the dialecticism which he felt was the essential method underlying sound strategy. We found that we had an almost identical view of how voters think about politics and what they currently felt about the political parties. In the months leading up to the 2005 general election he would phone me most weeks, usually with some particularly acute question in mind about a recent poll.

Later, when Philip was ill, we would sit on the green sofas in his home overlooking Regent's Park and for hours at a time debate the state of the parties and the mood of the country. By then the fates of our two parties, each with a new leader since Tony Blair's third election victory in 2005, had started to move in opposite directions.

One of the clearest lessons of *The Unfinished Revolution* is that, in the end, achieving modernisation required a party leader who believed in it. So it proved with the Conservatives.

David Cameron's hustings speech at the Tory conference in October 2005 electrified the party activists and transformed his candidacy instantly from outsider to prohibitive favourite. It was a speech delivered to great effect without notes, but it's real significance lay in a remarkably direct call for party modernisation. Cameron presented the party with an honest analysis of why it was still in opposition and defined a path of 'fundamental change' so that 'when we fight the next election ... we have a message that is relevant to people's lives today, that shows we're comfortable with modern Britain and that we believe our best days lie ahead'. He sought and won a mandate to modernise.

David Cameron showed how uncompromising his modernising agenda was in another, much less noticed, speech shortly after he'd won the leadership. In a public meeting in Chippenham a man in the audience asked if Cameron agreed that 'political correctness is ruining Britain' – to predictable rapturous applause from the audience of *Daily Mail* true-believers. David Cameron gave what one newspaper report described as 'a fierce riposte': 'In some ways,' he said, 'political correctness is a good thing. I don't want my disabled son to be called a spastic. I don't want my black neighbours to be called negroes, or a gay friend to be labelled queer.'

This was a direct challenge to a common default among Conservatives that was also a major reason why the party had seemed to many voters so old-fashioned and ill at ease in modern Britain: obsession with old taboos and contempt for new ones.

Philip Gould recognised almost at once that David Cameron 'got it' in a way that his predecessors had not – as, reportedly, did Tony Blair. More to the point, most voters felt the same. The party's headline support jumped from its twelve-year flatline of 32 per cent to 38 per cent in the month following Cameron's election as leader. The party's private polling and focus groups told the same story. For the first time since 1997 a clear majority of voters felt that the Conservative Party was changing for the better.

The modernising momentum did not relent. It is impossible to imagine any previous Conservative leader riding a dog-sled to see first-hand the melting Norwegian glaciers, as Cameron did in the first six months of his leadership. In his very first speech to the Tory conference as party leader, in October 2006, he spoke of his belief in 'liberal Conservatism'. In his second, three days later, he spoke of his belief in the importance of marriage, 'whether you're a man and a woman, a woman and a woman or a man and another man'. He explicitly identified the NHS as his single most important priority.

It was a decontamination focused on the party's specific weaknesses, just as Gould's modernisation of Labour had been. Old Labour's core vulnerability was economic. The Conservative root problem was the perception of its character – 'the nasty party'. Where the Blairites concentrated above all on persuading people that New Labour could be trusted to run the economy, the Cameroon focus was on showing that his values were 'modern and compassionate'. Conceptually it was the same process of understanding and connecting with changed values – of marrying core political values to a modern society much different from the last time the party was in power.

With determined modernising leadership, the Conservative Party made up for lost time, but winning outright in 2010 was always going to be hard. Had Conservative Party modernisation started sooner we would not have been starting such a long way back; going into the 2010 election the Tories still had fewer MPs than Labour had at their nadir, under Michael Foot. As it was, the Conservatives gained 100 seats, the most in any election since 1932 and won 2 million more votes than at the previous election. The 5 per cent swing in their favour was the third highest since the Second World War.

Right-wing revisionism now claims that the Conservatives should have won outright in 2010 – and would have done so but for modernisation. A Conservative overall majority was there for the taking, it is said, if only the leadership had pressed harder with robust Tory messages on tax and Europe and, above all, immigration; if, in other words, it had refought its 2005 campaign or its 2001 campaign. No evidence is ever offered in support of the assertion. It is the chorus of a cadre of culturally estranged Tory activists committing what Michael Portillo has described as 'the worst error you can make in politics': to presume that the electorate thinks the same as you.

The fact is that as the 2010 election campaign began, our private polling gave the Conservative Party a 39 per cent lead over Labour as best party on immigration. It clearly wasn't the key variable in the minds of floating voters. Most people had a strong, ingrained, belief that the Conservatives would inevitably be tougher on immigration than Labour. If we had made immigration a central campaign issue we might perhaps have stretched our lead on the issue to 45 per cent or 50 per cent. It is undoubtedly an important issue to many people. But all evidence shows that there are very few voters for whom it is *so* important as to decide which party they vote for – and almost all of them were already Conservative voters; virtually everyone else who ranked it their greatest concern were people who for other, usually tribal, reasons wouldn't vote Tory whatever we said about immigration.

The 2005 Conservative campaign had already tested to destruction the notion that making immigration a dominant message was the route to victory. Michael Ashcroft's investment in detailed daily tracking polling, published after the election in his book *Smell the Coffee: A Wake-up Call to the Conservative Party*, proved beyond doubt that it was the prominence of the party's message on immigration that drove away swathes of middle-class potential Tory voters.

The doubt that most floating voters had about the Conservatives in 2010 was not that we wouldn't be better than Labour on immigration. Nor was it about David Cameron; it was the rest of the party that was the problem.

People could see that Cameron was a different kind of Conservative – a compassionate, modern, family man – and one who possessed the vital, elusive x-factor of leadership. People liked him and the idea of him. As people who had never voted Conservative before wrestled with the thought, what held them back was their perception of the wider Tory party. He was a modernising leader, but had his party truly modernised? Did they really want to be led where he obviously wanted to take them?

It is the orthodox view of political historians that the Tory party's greatest facet through the years has been its ability to change. This is the attribute that made the British Conservative Party one of the most successful parties in the world and the dominant party of the twentieth century – which, in Philip Gould's analysis, should have been Labour's because it was an era defined by a shift in power from the privileged to the people. 'The Conservatives stole the people's century from Labour', he wrote, 'because they modernised while Labour did not.' But somehow, during the nervous breakdown that afflicted the Tory party after the defenestration of Margaret Thatcher, a lot of Conservatives lost the knack for change. Michael Portillo – himself one of the inner circle of loyalists who went to Number 10 the night before she resigned and begged her to fight on – thinks that 'the most important thing about Mrs Thatcher is that she was at the cutting edge of change', as befits someone who had defined 'people and how they want to live their lives' as the most important force in politics. For how people want to live their lives inevitably changes. As Disraeli said, in a remark cited by Philip Gould in *The Unfinished Revolution*, 'Change is inevitable in a progressive country. Change is constant.' This was the heart of the Gould theory of political strategy: change is constant; the revolution is always unfinished. You can only go forward, never back.

The day after the 2010 election Philip sent me an email saying simply: 'They didn't change enough. If they had, they would have stormed it.'

A year later, when David Cameron asked me to join his team in Downing Street, I wondered if it was the right thing to do and whether a pollster was inherently of more value advising from outside, as Philip had always done. Over tea and fruitcake in his Cotswolds retreat – and by then seriously ill again – he kindly and patiently encouraged me and reassured my even more doubtful wife.

Our final few emails debated the exact complexion of the current, strange, political mood. Philip agreed with my conclusion that most voters had come to terms with and internalised the need for austerity. His very last email to me observed that the public 'are moving to a new place, in an odd way rather as I am, accepting the reality, not fighting it'. 'But you do', he ended, 'also need hope and optimism.' Nothing could better sum up the man and his view of politics. Philip Gould's final word to me: optimism.

A US Perspective on 'The Philip Gould Project'

10

Stanley B. Greenberg

Even as Bill Clinton settled into a large lead over President George Bush after his nominating convention, the core team in Little Rock kept gaming out how we could still lose. Pretending I was Bob Teeter, Bush's pollster, I conducted a national survey in order to design the best campaign possible against Bill Clinton; our media team made simulated ads and we used the survey to test our response. The resulting 'Teeter Memo' proposed that Bush lead off with an attack ad, 'Bill Clinton, failed governor of a small state', and close the campaign on 'trust'. But instead, the real Bush campaign, doubtful that the country would elect a 'draft dodger' as President, stayed on the Vietnam War draft even though the voters were done with it. That misreading would lead voters to lock in for Clinton.

My biggest remaining worry was that voters, for all their developing comfort for Bill Clinton and desire for change, would hesitate come Election Day, blocked by memories of a Democratic Party long associated with high taxes, welfare and overspending, weakness on national security, and an inability to represent working people. This was no idle worry, given what had happened with the Labour Party in Britain earlier that year. They too had a poll lead going into Election Day, but the Conservatives won and won pretty handily.

I met Philip Gould many years earlier on one of his trips to the US. He was gathering every bit of information he could on US campaigns and, occasionally, recruiting consultants to come help the Labour Party; and I had met Jonathan Powell from the British

Embassy earlier in the year who came to my office in Washington to learn as much as he could about New Democrats, like Bill Clinton.

So, with the Labour Party defeat in my mind, I decided to invite Philip to come to Little Rock to meet with James Carville, George Stephanopoulos, the media people and myself – those who formed the core War Room team – so he could lay out what went wrong at the end. What role did unaddressed, nagging doubts about the Labour Party play in their defeat? Were the Democrats similarly at risk? What could we learn from their experience?

Philip wrote, 'I received a memo from [Greenberg's] office which read: "Stan is anxious to meet you here in Little Rock, Arkansas, at the Clinton Campaign Headquarters. We are anxious to have you observe the campaign, and to hear about your efforts."' Philip described the fax as life-changing, 'water in the desert', and he jumped on the first plane he could.[1] In retrospect, it was a turning point that allowed Philip – and the two of us to collaborate – to change the way progressive parties battle and actually win.

Little Rock is not easy to get to. While Philip was working his way across the country, the Bush campaign shopped a story about Clinton travelling to Moscow during the Vietnam War to renounce his citizenship. They also distributed to TV stations an effective ad on how Clinton's promises would raise your taxes – in British-speak, their 'tax bombshell'. Somebody made the connection that the Conservatives in Britain had loaned their media consultants to the Bush campaign, which, might now be plagiarising its language as Joe Biden once did with a Neil Kinnock speech. We rushed Philip into a press briefing in order to blow up their ads and create a lot of smoke, an action which put the Bush people on the defensive.[2] In this new era of rapid response, Philip earned his stripes and respect all around. He ended up staying four weeks to observe, indeed to ensconce himself in the War Room with the response team while we were off 'prepping' for the three presidential debates.

I had no idea then how big a role Philip was playing with Labour's potential modernising leaders, but he was utterly shameless in stealing the techniques that we introduced. I do not underestimate the importance of left parties feeling confident of their ability to guide the agenda and win, showing voters strength and a capacity to govern. My partner James Carville was a big part of that, as he was the force behind the War Room's open internal culture and ruthless, rapid response that changed campaigns forever. Philip would bring the War Room and rapid response to Millbank Tower, the Labour Party headquarters, with the actual floor and desk plan from Little Rock taped on the wall.

Far more important than our campaign's techniques is 'the project' that gave it purpose and direction. What I did not realise at the time was that Philip was reading my work on a Democratic Party that I described as 'short on patriotism, weak on defense, soft on criminals and minorities, indifferent to work, values and the family, and inexplicably infatuated with taxes'. I had alienated almost everyone within the established party and the Democratic National Committee – except, fortunately, for Bill Clinton, who embraced my 'Middle Class Project' that 'the Democrats need to reassert their claim to represent the majority of working Americans'.[3]

Philip came back from his Clinton experience determined even more to change the Labour Party, and even more brutal in his critique of his own party's failure to face fully the history and public distrust on spending, inflation, taxes, the trade unions, and crime. Others, like Margaret McDonagh who would head the general election campaign and eventually the Labour Party, had also enlisted in the Clinton effort and learned many of the same lessons. In Philip's words, they needed to move the party to 'focus on hard-working people and their concerns'.[4]

To the great discomfort of many in the Labour Party, including John Smith, the leader in that period before the ascent of Tony Blair and Gordon Brown, Philip invited a group of us from the Clinton campaign to come to a one-day conference at the Queen Elizabeth Conference Centre in Westminster. I am sure we were pretty arrogant at that point, and our separate meeting with Smith could not have been chillier.[5]

Philip and I stayed in touch when I was pollster to President Clinton, and I got the White House to agree to a formal 'exchange programme' between the Democratic Party and the Labour Party – despite the fact that John Major was still the British Prime Minister. Philip came to observe our focus groups, and he talked about my getting involved in Britain. In fact, Sidney Blumenthal invited my wife, Congresswoman Rosa DeLauro, and me to a small dinner at his house with Tony Blair. Blair and I sat next to each other, and I tried to get a feel for whether Blair was another Bill Clinton. Blair wanted to know whether Bill Clinton was going to be successful, something not at all certain in 1993, with implications for the modernisers.

After Blair became leader of the Labour Party, Philip convinced Blair, Alastair Campbell and Peter Mandelson that I should take over the Labour Party polling programme. They were 20 points ahead of the Conservatives in the polls, but Philip truly took nothing for granted.

I first came to observe some of Philip's focus groups in the spring of 1995 and got my introduction to Philip's methods on his home turf, in his own style, even though I was supposed to be a kind of 'guru' in this type of research. We went to Edgware for groups with 'Tory switchers'.[6] As a moderator, Philip had an intimate and engaged relationship with the participants, unlike the more detached style I ask facilitators to use. Before long, Philip engaged in spirited debate with the participants, even arguing with them at points, but in such a way that brought out underlying thinking and points of resistance. He was not a partisan, like a Frank Luntz, but tried to see how far the argument would play out. Philip got his energy from that engagement, but also his authority when making the case with Blair or the team. He was the one who understood the way people thought through these issues, and the leader turned to him for his frank, unvarnished observations.

Sometimes Philip would get on the phone with Blair while in the car back from groups, or even hand me the phone for my response, but he still always got a note to him by morning. The topic was invariably what we have to do to get heard or reach our goal; never what position to take.

When I conducted focus groups during Clinton's first two years as President, I viewed my research, in particular the postcards people wrote to the President at the end of each focus group, as a way of getting ordinary people heard in political circles often deaf to popular opinion. Philip conducted these groups every week and during the campaigns every night; he really was the voice of those people. He respected them – and continuously made them part of the decision-making at the highest levels. To this day, I can see the faces of many of those participants and hear their anguished calls and hopes for change – and Philip was with them. During the campaigns, we would sometimes do groups with people who participated previously, and you could see the familiarity and bond as we grappled with what held them back or why they finally decided. On election eve, we would speak with people who had done multiple groups and it was more a party than a group, with a fair amount of wine consumed. He had real bond with voters and gave them a voice. He was uncynical about the voter.

Philip was never embarrassed by being a pollster or the idea that elites should pay attention to polls and people. Over time, he came to a subtle appreciation for how voters form, hold, and change judgements. 'Most people will make an assumption, and will hold that assumption, despite countervailing evidence, until something tips or something snaps.' When it changes, it happens collectively. 'Before every election there is a moment when the public seem to decide in unison not only what the election is about but what the words are that define it.'[7]

After observing that first set of groups in 1995 and reviewing their existing poll results, I had my first meeting in Britain with Blair and the team and wrote my first Labour memo.

What stood out for me was how close to the surface was Labour's history of the last 25 years, even as they were intrigued but still sceptical about Blair. We forget now that voters then described him as 'smarmy', the same way voters described Bill Clinton as 'slick' – a politician 'just telling you what you want to hear'. I told Blair and his advisers that 'voters need relentless reassurance'. That was unsurprising, but they were ready for a second and third opinion on a strategy they would take all the way to the general election. I joined the effort, and before we were done, I had moved my entire polling team from America to the War Room in England, computers and all, and when I was lucky enough to predict the final vote at 43 per cent to 31 per cent – to the point – I got permission to stay.

Philip threw me into the centre of decision-making because he thought it would help Labour win against what he considered great historic odds. I am not naive, and I know Philip left some wreckage along the way – frayed relationships that he came to regret. But he was so determined that Labour and New Labour be successful that he took everything I would give and made sure I was meeting with Blair, whether at his house, at Downing Street, or Chequers. Philip clearly had his own theory of the case, but at key moments, he gave me the field to myself. I took that for granted at the time, but not now.

Philip and I began in similar places at different times and moved to similar conclusions at perhaps a different pace and in different ways, both informed by continuous research with people, but our thinking and project was pretty closely aligned. We did not fight about our emerging conclusions and recommendations, and with his new and final writings, I believe we are aligned on how to advance the project now.

For a decade starting in the late 1980s, the New Democrats and Bill Clinton had the stage, showing that a modernised Democratic Party could win election – and re-election. We showed that you could transcend the struggles and interests of the industrial and counter-cultural periods and offer a centre-left party relevant to changing times. But when the Republicans took control of the US Congress from 1994 onwards, President Clinton faced extraordinary challenges. It is amazing what he accomplished in that period, including welfare reform, a balanced budget and strong economic growth. By contrast, Tony Blair and New Labour had the opportunity to govern with a huge parliamentary majority to bring change and advance a new centre-left model. When Bill Clinton visited Number 10, he asked whether he could borrow some of those seats.

Neither Philip nor I would be there but for Bill Clinton and Tony Blair. They exploited both of us because we were the carriers and shapers of the project of modernising our respective parties so they could represent the majority of working people, broadly defined. They empowered us, even as they brought many other considerations to campaigning and governance. We were given the mandate to do it together in the big election of 1997 and, even more, 2001. Philip was at the heart of Blair's campaign to win a second full term, the significance for Labour of which he understood more than me.

Our partnership in advancing the centre-left project reached beyond the US and Britain. Few people probably realise that we worked together intensively in the election of Gerhard Schroeder as Chancellor of Germany; Schroeder underscored his openness to business and, therefore, changing his own party. So too did we combine our efforts for a time in the election of Ehud Barak as Prime Minister of Israel, Israel's most decorated soldier, who reassured voters they could trust the left on security. Around our continuing project, Philip and I formed a business that had some important corporate clients, but the heart of our collaboration was working to change centre-left parties and enabling them to win. We shared an office overlooking the Thames and St Paul's Cathedral in the Express Building, in a partnership with Clive Hollick and NOP.

I think how casually I use the word 'project' in describing what about Philip changed the fortunes and character of the Labour Party. But if you read the preface and conclusion of his first account of this transformation, he does not use the word, 'project'; rather it tells of the 'modernization of the Labour Party' with a bold thesis: 'Labour lost the twentieth century and allowed the Conservatives to govern for seventy of the last hundred years because it failed to modernise; it forgot the people it had been created for. It took the modernisers to save the Labour Party.'[8] The thesis was bold and right, even if the ambition for a 'progressive century' might be an overreach – though even now, the Conservatives are struggling to escape the new common sense created by New Labour.

By the time Philip wrote his new, extraordinary account of Tony Blair's time in government, its aftermath, and his expansive 'Letter to the Next Generation', Philip had embraced the term 'project' as the central lesson of this book, essentially of his life: 'Unless you base everything around a core political project then you will not achieve enduring success.' New Labour was 'such a project'.[9]

For Philip, 'strategy' is embedded in a project. It is *holistic*, 'seeking to shape and understand the entire political landscape'. It is not about any particular box, but 'it is making sense of all the boxes'. And it is about *fundamentals*, 'not what you see on the surface that matters but the underlying substance; not just what things are but what they may become'. Writing artfully, 'the world is a constellation of forces in motion, some emerging, some declining'.[10]

His much richer account recalls my own conclusion in *Dispatches from the War Room*, where I wrote about how all our tools – including reassurances about the past – can become 'mere tactics', absent the end goal of a serious political project. Without the 'prism of strategy', as he describes it, what we do can pretty easily descend into 'triangulation' or robbing opponents of their issues so they are politically naked or neutralised; or into trumpeting some micro-group, rather than seeing the holistic forces driving the future.[11] Because his polling work is embedded in a project, it bears no resemblance to the tracking polls published every day by YouGov in Britain or Gallup in the United States.

When I started writing this chapter, I presumed I would be writing about Philip Gould's influence and legacy – part of my own process for coming to terms with our unfinished relationship and his death. But what I came to realise in reading was that Philip, in anticipation of his own end, has written this amazing, fresh account of the great challenges facing Britain and the Labour Party now. I should have realised when we discussed Ed Miliband's conference speech just a month before Philip died from oesophageal cancer and offered such acute advice, that he was thinking about the future, not the past.

So I feel an obligation as one-half insider and one-half outsider to engage with his last writings with the same kind of spiritedness and honesty that Philip had for advancing his project and aiding all those who are struggling to win on the left in these difficult times.

Gordon Brown and Tony Blair: The Problem of Project

After putting down Blair's own account of the Labour government – *A Journey: My Political Life* – the biggest question I wanted to pose to him was how could he have not moved Brown out as Chancellor after the 2001 election. With all the dark accounts of their relationship, the internal conflicts and the amount of energy devoted to managing it on both sides, Blair could have advanced with his reform agenda much earlier and with greater clarity. In his closing writing, Philip still reminds us how much Blair and Brown accomplished together, but both Philip and Blair believed the most productive period for reforming how government works came in the final two years in office.

I do not highlight the Brown–Blair conflict to relive any of this, but to underscore what happens to Labour or any party when it lacks this kind of purpose and project. In the first Labour government, Brown was determined to restrain government spending and bring economic stability; he focused like a laser on tax credits and other measures that supported hardworking families, reduced poverty and ensured income gains were broad-based. But when he came to lead the Labour government in 2007, those ideas were exhausted. He played a historic, global role during the financial crisis of 2008–09 and masterfully drew dividing lines against the 'boom and bust' Tories who threatened frontline services in the 2010 election. But that is not a project.

For less than a month, I was deeply involved in the erstwhile and failed deliberations over whether the Prime Minister should call an early election. While I had not previously been part of Brown's team, I was apparently trusted in both camps and met frequently with Brown and the major players in his camp. I came to support calling the election and, for sure, thought he would win based on a series of national and marginal polls we conducted, though with a reduced parliamentary majority. Bob Shrum and I had dinner with Philip, and he could not have been clearer: this was a no-brainer. But Brown was unbelievably risk-averse.

But much more important, Brown was *project*-averse. What I discovered in trying to write the survey questionnaire and test themes and policy issues for a potential election, was that Brown had no project, no hidden agenda poised to unveil for a new Labour government. That would be all too evident when Brown chose to serve out the term and then lost disastrously in 2010.

Philip said it is even more important to have a project when in government. 'This is why a strong and serious project is so vital: the ideas, values, beliefs and policy that give meaning even in chaos and that made New Labour such a potent and sustained political force.'[12] When that faltered, Labour faltered.

The Conservatives' Lack of Project Seriously Damages Their Fortunes

At numerous points in Philip's 'Letter to the Next Generation', he talks about the Conservatives failing to change their party sufficiently, and indeed lack of a project anything like the scale of New Labour. Cameron seemed to take the rough edges off the party, but he changed his own image more than his party. And every day the Liberal Democrats try to show they are responsible for the good things in the coalition, they reinforce the point: Conservatives are unchanged. The dramatic poll fall after the budget this year just underscores that the Conservatives are still a 36 per cent party. No amount of reassurance or language will save them if there is no new project to motivate their advance.

The one time that the government moved to about 40 per cent of the vote came after David Cameron's veto of the new European Union treaty to rescue the euro at the end of 2011.[13] Their vote was drawn from UKIP and Eurosceptic voters, which suggests another route for them getting to a parliamentary majority. Still, absent a project to give direction and confidence, they could pay a price among those who have warmed to a supposedly more open Conservative Party. Again, project matters.

Tony Blair's Personal and Political Projects

At the end of his 'Letter to the Next Generation', Philip writes, 'There are really two Tony Blairs out there, the private and the public, connected but separate.' And at the heart of Blair is a 'central contradiction' – 'a tension between the world of values that ultimately drives him and the world of politics he has chosen to inhabit'. Philip admits, 'It took the years of illness to allow me to discover this.'[14] That is a big conclusion, and Philip did not have time to play out the implications.

When I wrote my memoir and reflected about Blair and interviewed him, I moved to the same conclusion about what I called his 'political project' and 'his personal mission'. My conclusion did not come when I was on a personal journey, like Philip, but it was only in retrospect when I was trying to understand the political leaders I had worked for: 'I came to work for Blair at the point when the political project and his mission met in which the electoral task forced a kind of consistency, evident at the end in 1997, 2001, and 2005', I wrote. 'At near dawn, when he claimed victory, however, he always pulled them apart', affirming that both would guide his actions in the years ahead.[15]

I have even deeper respect for Tony Blair as a consequence of understanding that tension. In my book, I am mostly critical of our own team, including myself, for not embracing that as part of our message task. If this were a presidential election you could not run authentically without making that part of your identity and purpose. But the truth is the team was consumed with the political project of New Labour and reluctant to put centre-stage Blair's communitarian thinking: individualism needing a strong community, unity over divisiveness, rooted above all in his faith. But to be clear, Blair too was unsure how far he wanted to go, as he was simultaneously pragmatic, which produced an unending re-evaluation of our purpose.

When I conducted my first surveys for Labour prior to the conference speech in 1995, the strongest message drafted with the team and Philip began: 'The Labour Party seeks to put hard working families back at the centre of civic life in Britain.' The strongest characterisations of the Tories were: 'don't care about the ordinary person', 'on the side of the rich and powerful', and 'Tories did not govern for all'. All the reform language, like 'renew', tested dreadfully. Based on the results, Philip prepared a PowerPoint for Blair, but Blair decided to anchor the speech instead on 'One Nation', something we had not even tested. Philip rushed to throw on some groups to see what to make of it, but Blair insisted that it be the organising theme.

Blair began his conference speech talking about socialism's essential meaning: 'It is a moral purpose to life; a set of values.' It is 'a belief in society, in cooperation, in achieving together what we are unable to achieve alone'. Unapologetically, he said, 'I am my brother's keeper' and said the basic principles of my politics: we are 'members of the same family, same community, the same human race'.[16]

That is where he tried to go repeatedly – and even when I struggled to stretch with Philip's help to a synthetic contrast – 'a Labour Party prepared to represent the whole nation and a Conservative Party that aspires to aid only the richest and most powerful'. It did not move him – and as a consequence we were barely able to formulate a distinct, unified economic narrative in an election that would centre on economic competence.

Philip would remember that we presented to some focus groups Blair's speech on the 'stakeholder economy' and, to be honest, their eyes glazed over. I wrote on my pad, 'not listening', as it did not relate to their pain and motivating critique. I wrote in a note to Blair as we were moving closer to the election, 'This is not about overcoming divisions and uniting the country'; 'this is about a Labour vision that says the country should work for everyone, not just the privileged few'. Concluding, I wrote, 'This is the core premise of the one nation idea, and we seem to be losing it.'[17]

Finally, and in his way in the final conference speech before the election, Blair said that the Tories were content with 'a 30–40–30' – 30 per cent 'doing very well', 30 per cent 'just getting by' and 40 per cent 'struggling or worse'. It was Blair's view of a two-tier Britain, and allowed him to pose the choice: 'For all the people. Or for a few.' He took it to Major: 'What kind of world is it where the best education, the best jobs, the best skills, are available only to the few?' Getting to the election, he redefined two-tier Britain in his own expansive, non-divisive moral terms. He was big on winning, to be sure, but he relished winning with support 'flat' in class terms, gaining as high a percentage with professionals and upper-middle-class voters (ABs), as with working-class and poorer ones, even if the latter fell off significantly.

Philip and I, in real time and in reflection, believed the 'Forces of Conservatism' conference speech more than two years into his term was his strongest ever. Blair offered as the main critique: 'The country has run far too long on the talents of the few, when the genius of the many lies uncared for, and ignored.' Writing in his 'Letter to the Next Generation', Philip says, 'In many ways it was this particular speech that Blair really began to find his voice.' In reflection, he found it more subtle and nuanced than the reaction at the time, as 'it was a defence of solidarity and community, modernisation and, above all, progressive politics'. He concludes, it was 'another step forward for the definition of New Labour and Blairism'.[18]

When I saw Blair after the speech at the family and friends reception, I embraced him and lauded the speech. But let us be honest: some in the inner circle immediately described it as divisive, offensive toward former Tory voters, and alienating of business who thought New Labour was a big tent. And the Murdoch press hated the speech.

To buttress the speech, both Philip and I wrote notes; Philip saying, do not 'be deflected or unnerved' by the opposition. I went further in my memo marked 'urgent' and entitled 'The New Strategic

World: Opportunities for Hegemony'. I said we are no longer about the past, 'The speech at Bournemouth was so important because it promised a new Labour project motivated by the passion to liberate every individual to realize their potential and by a struggle against the forces of conservatism that stifle opportunity, except for the few.' Blair said the memo was brilliant, and David Miliband wrote, 'really powerful indeed: moving us from "triangulation" against Old Labour and the Tories to a "bipolarity" against the Tories', which 'is immensely challenging but right'.[19]

I underscore the speech because Philip and I lost the argument. Blair did not go back to it – even as the campaign team, including Campbell, repeatedly asked, why not just go back to 'the forces of conservatism?'[20]

As we were trying to build back support a year before the 2005 elections, I met with Blair in a small study at Chequers to share the results of a poll that included a message he wrote: 'We stand for traditional British values – fairness, obligations to others, creative talent, but have the courage to apply them in a new way for the world.' The message that dominated everything was, 'We are working to change Britain so that in a modern and uncertain world, hardworking people, not just the few, have the opportunity to make a better life.' The message was 15 points weaker, I pointed out, when you excised 'not just the few'. He never liked using the term 'hardworking families' and looked like I was offering a pact with the devil, and told me frankly, 'I just don't believe the problem with Britain is the few at the top.'

In a note to the senior aides, Blair was uncharacteristically blunt, 'the big tent will be our approach' and 'everybody should get on board'. When I asked later why he did not fire us, he said, 'You were giving me the right advice for an election. It's just that I was choosing not to take it.'[21]

In first edition of *The Unfinished Revolution*, in the very final paragraph, Philip affirmed that a successful progressive politics means that 'the great majority of working people are helped and helped and supported by the Labour Party, not now and again, but again and again. That is why the Labour Party was formed.'[22]

He just presumed that was at the heart of what Blair wanted as well, and with enough effort, we would get to the same place, and he was mostly right.[23]

When we got into the actual campaign, Blair always found a way of getting closer to the team's advice, brilliantly introducing Thatcher in 2001 as a way of raising powerfully the underlying fears about the Tories contained in our message, as headlined in our posters: 'Be afraid. Be very afraid', as William Hague morphed into Margaret Thatcher.

New Labour as History: Immigration, Income Decline and Inequality

I embrace Philip's notion that successful parties are constantly renewing, modernising and embracing change and the future. Working with him, observing and reading his writings now bring home how few people get to do what we do, through multiple generations of leaders and activists. But at what point does the history we helped create (and we fell short) become part of the problem that successive generations have to address? I wish I could have posed this question to Philip directly, as it became clearer to me only when writing this chapter.

In Blair's preface to the new edition and Philip's note to the next generation, they struggle with how to deal with immigration – how to recognise the legitimacy of the worries, without making Britain inward-looking or giving into prejudice. In truth, I watched Blair as Prime Minister try to deal with asylum-seekers, when most members of his own government were extremely reluctant to address the flow or what was happening in council housing. By contrast, Brown thought addressing crime and asylum put us onto Tory territory and that would hurt Labour in the election. Philip always thought it was a critical task and described how voters' 'concerns about immigration continued to heighten, and it was increasingly seen as a primary cause of other problems'.[24]

When I conducted independent focus groups during the 2010 election and a post-election survey, it was hard to understate the level of anger about immigration – immigration and benefit, immigration and public spending, immigration and crime. In voters' views, Labour on its watch over many years had lost control of immigration, with major consequences for the country and living standards of working people.[25] The hardworking people that we are to represent were also losing ground economically over the last half-decade before Labour lost in 2010, even as executive compensation and incomes of the top 1 per cent surged.

Philip defended Labour's record on inequality, showing that between 1996 and 2010 every quintile gained 1.5–2.0 per cent – very different from the story under the previous Conservative governments. But as Philip knew better than anyone, real people do not make judgements in that way. In the last five years of Labour governance, incomes fell for the bottom 15 per cent, and grew by less than 1 per cent for everyone, except the top 15 per cent of earners.[26] We know that the same happened in the US and other countries, but that is not important for people. They were losing ground under Labour, even as they thought Labour was losing control in other ways.

When I first met with Tony Blair in 1995, I talked about the need for relentless reassurance about Labour's history. Then, it was about unions, spending and taxes. Of course, those issues are still important. But in a period of increasing globalisation and integration with Europe and stagnant or declining incomes, core constituencies for Labour have legitimate questions about whether in government we protected and promoted the British people. That very worry is at the heart of elections across Europe, with fragmentation of support away from mainstream parties of the right and left.

The next generation of leaders needs to embrace Labour's history in funding and renewing frontline public services, but doesn't it also have to acknowledge what happened with income gains, inequality and immigration? Do they need to relentlessly show they 'get it'?

Had Philip lived to advise the next Labour government, which he told Andrew Marr was his hope, I am pretty confident he would have moved to these issues because he was already grappling with them. He was focused increasingly in the last year or two on the changes taking place globally, 'so fast-moving, so complex, so fragmented that events would emerge which would be hard to predict, destructive in their impact and sometimes irreversible in their consequences'. He was very focused on the decreasing inequality among nations, accompanied inexorably by inequality here, with growing pressure on lower- and middle-income groups. 'Two sides of the world, two faces of globalisation, two conceptions of fairness – huge global trends articulated by families who may never meet but who always be some way be joined.'

And his appreciation for what globalisation produced meant that we face 'new issues of fairness', 'a real and growing social aspiration that will not be abated'. That is why he aligned himself with Will Hutton's statement: 'the more capitalism adopts fair process, the better it works'. He went further: 'only fair economies and societies will be genuinely sustainable. This is the battleground for the next great struggle in politics.'[27]

Battling to finish his argument on his last day of holiday, he wrote what he now considered the essence of New Labour:

> To shape this future we need strategies that can accept contradiction and resolve them; to know that our purpose in politics is to turn values into change; to understand that the sustainable creation of wealth requires fairness; and that hope and aspiration are at the heart of progressive politics. The instinctive desire to look at the world not as it is, but as it can be.[28]

I know Philip was writing for his family, for his colleagues, for the next generation and for Britain, but I learned from his work and feel renewed in advancing the project that I feel determined to carry on.

Notes

1. Philip Gould, *The Unfinished Revolution: How New Labour Changed British Politics For Ever*, 2nd edn (Little, Brown, 2011), p. 158.
2. Philip Gould, *The Unfinished Revolution: How the Modernisers Saved the Labour Party* (Little, Brown, 1998), pp. 162–170.

3. Gould, *Unfinished Revolution* (1998), pp. 171–174.
4. Gould, *Unfinished Revolution* (1998), pp. 176–77.
5. See my account in Stanley B. Greenberg, *Dispatches from the War Room: In the Trenches with Five Extraordinary Leaders* (St. Martin's Press, 2009), pp. 181–182.
6. Greenberg, *Dispatches from the War Room*, pp. 188–191.
7. Gould, *Unfinished Revolution* (2011), pp. 419–420.
8. Gould, *Unfinished Revolution* (1998), p. xii.
9. Gould, *Unfinished Revolution* (2011), p. 403.
10. Gould, *Unfinished Revolution* (2011), p. 406.
11. Greenberg, *Dispatches from the War Room*, pp. 423–429.
12. Gould, *Unfinished Revolution* (2011), pp. 406–407.
13. Ian Traynor, Nicholas Watt, David Gow and Patrick Wintour, 'David Cameron blocks EU treaty with veto, casting Britain adrift in Europe', *Guardian,* 9 December 2011, http://www.guardian.co.uk/world/2011/dec/09/david-cameron-blocks-eu-treaty
    Average of polls from UK Polling Report (http://ukpollingreport.co.uk/voting-intention), 11–17 December 2011.
14. Gould, *Unfinished Revolution* (2011), pp. 525–526.
15. Greenberg, *Dispatches from the War Room*, pp. 415–416.
16. Greenberg, *Dispatches from the War Room*, pp. 194–96.
17. Greenberg, *Dispatches from the War Room*, pp. 204–209.
18. Gould, *Unfinished Revolution* (2011), pp. 436–437.
19. Greenberg, *Dispatches from the War Room*, pp. 225–227.
20. Greenberg, *Dispatches from the War Room*, p. 231.
21. Greenberg, *Dispatches from the War Room*, p. 234.
22. Gould, *Unfinished Revolution*, 1998, p. 399.
23. Gould, *Unfinished Revolution*, 2011, p. 514.
24. Gould, *Unfinished Revolution*, 2011, pp. 492–493.
25. From Greenberg Quinlan Rosner pre-election focus groups (February and March 2010). Public polling also showed immigration's importance and the perception of Labour mishandling. An Angus Reid poll (1 April 2010) found 75 per cent of Britons believed that the Labour Party's immigration policy over the last 13 years was a 'failure'.
26. Robert Joyce et al., *Poverty and Inequality in UK: 2010* (Institute for Fiscal Studies, May 2010), p. 26, http://www.ifs.org.uk/comms/comm116.pdf
27. Gould, *Unfinished Revolution* (2011), pp. 532–534.
28. Gould, *Unfinished Revolution* (2011), p. 538.

Life in the 'Death Zone'

11

James Harding

When Philip Gould pitched the idea of writing for *The Times* on his time with cancer, it sounded as if he was sketching out another political memo. His party had, at the time, let him down. The Conservatives were back in power, enjoying the easy press that comes with the first months of office. And Philip Gould's cancer story offered what he saw as a powerful morality tale that showed the shortcomings of private healthcare against the world-beating treatment of the National Health Service. He had fought his whole life for the NHS. For the past two years, it had kept him alive. He had found the perfect focus group for the New Labour argument of public service values versus private sector efficiency. The focus group happened to be him.

He knew, too, that his story had a cast of political characters whose care and affection for each other in private had rarely been glimpsed before in public. The scenes around the bedside, he said, featured the extraordinary conversations he had had with 'Tony', 'Alastair' and 'Gordon' too. Philip was savvy enough to know that, in his casual reference to the central figures of the New Labour decade, he was describing an unusual hospital drama.

But all these were the trimmings. The meat of what Philip proposed was a serious reflection on his battle with cancer. It was to be much more meaningful than another political memo. He did not tell me exactly what he would say, except that he would tell 'all of it'. He was not promising newfound religion (although we would, in time, come to that) nor some deathbed spirituality. But listening to him talk, as ever, excitedly about this next big unfeasible project, it was clear that he had in mind an inspirational account of his time with a terminal illness. That sounded like a characteristically Gouldian undertaking. It would involve the tackling of a taboo in a spirit of optimism. Typically, too, it would be framed without pretensions to a philosophy, but in practical terms. Like so much of Philip's thinking, it would seem surprising on the first reading, but like common sense on the second.

It was also offered up with a sense of the moment. He wrote his reflections on his battle with cancer at a time when the country was, in a host of ways, reappraising its relationship with death. It is hard to judge when a culture crosses a threshold, even with the benefit of hindsight. It is even harder to do so at the time. But in the first decade of the twenty-first century, there was an upheaval under way in public attitudes to dying. There was growing interest – and increasing sympathy – for the small number of terminally ill people, who, accompanied by their friends or their families, were making the journey to a drab clinic in Switzerland to end their lives. The BBC dramatised one such story and it starred Julie Walters – she was the heroine, rather than the villain of the piece. In fact, the debate about Dignitas was dominated not by calls that the Swiss service should be shut down, but consideration of whether it should be legally replicated in Britain. Meanwhile, Debbie Purdy had been in the High Court, seeking to secure the indemnity of her husband in the event that he took her life, with her consent, when her illness became unbearable. And in the House of Lords, too, Lord Joffe had been seeking to provide limited protections for those involved in specific instances in assisted dying. In the argument between sanctity of life and dignity in death, the balance was tipping. In politics, Philip had a knack for putting into words the unspoken drift of popular thinking. At the end of his life, he found himself pointing the way to a new accommodation with death. If he did not set the direction of national opinion, he certainly seemed to recognise it.

Philip had an optimist's outlook. *The Unfinished Revolution*, his account of the making of New Labour published the year after Tony Blair came to power, had not only made the positive case for politics to improve the country. It offered – as he always did – an exciting, enthusiastic idea of a modern Britain. Ten years later, when we met up to talk about the 2010 general election, this was again Philip's theme: who would offer an inspiring idea of what it would mean to be British in 2015 or, say, 2020. The prospect of Philip writing about terminal cancer was extraordinary, in part, because it was the ultimate test of his optimism.

Looking back on the notes we exchanged as he worked on the piece for *The Times*, I am reminded of what a happy business this was. The exchanges we had were affectionate. We signed off our emails to each other with notes of admiration from me, words of encouragement from him. And I smile, too, with embarrassment. For weeks, it seemed, I was chivvying him to file. (It sounded good, I wanted it in the paper.) And he was apologising for the delay, promising it would land any day now. (He was undergoing chemotherapy.)

Here is the note he sent me on 30 March:

> It is almost the end of March and I wanted to update you on progress. I have so far written 26,000 words which I am pretty amazed by given how ill I have been feeling! This is of course far too long and I am cutting it down to around 10,000 words for you. I will keep it long because there are so many stories and you will know best which to keep and which to discard. I can assure you that there are many 'locked in the cupboard' moments. Far too many probably for my own reputation. I have written it as a chronological narrative with several themes flowing from it: personal spiritual and political. It also contains a portrait of Tony B that is unlike anything ever written about him before. The piece is completely honest and exposes me somewhat but I am convinced it is the right thing to do. So have a little patience. I will get a draft over to you pretty soon – days not weeks. But I am always a bit slower than I hope I will be ...

He signed off, typically, with a fillip – an unwarranted compliment and a word of support for the line the paper was taking on Libya. I remember feeling awed by his energy, impressed by his commitment to the project and, to be blunt, a little worried. It is always a risk commissioning a piece from someone you know and like, as the rules still apply: if it is boring, if it is self-indulgent, if it is muddled, it is not going in the paper. And, whereas it's always possible to rewrite or write through a thousand words and make it work, that's not the case for 26,000 words. Nor did I know exactly where we would put all those words. A long magazine feature rarely runs longer than 4,000 words. The entire run of news pages, home and foreign, would only just accommodate all that Philip was writing. I had not discussed the project with anyone else at the paper and, as it became clear that Philip was not writing an article but the better part of a book, I wondered (a) whether it would be printable, and (b) where we would put it.

I think that is the reason why, when it landed at the end of May, I procrastinated for a day about reading it. I needn't have worried. He had called it 'The Glory of the Ride', a phrase he had picked up off a T-shirt he had been given by his daughters when he went to New York for surgery. It was a title that may have obscured the subject, but it certainly nailed the spirit. It was stirring and searching, veering between passages of practical storytelling and then moments of uplifting observation on hope, pain and fear. It had plainly been worked on with meticulous care: no typos, no repetitions, no mess. Philip's passion for things could sometimes mean that when he spoke, his thinking was a scatter-gun, multi-directional affair; in his writing, he was still heartfelt, but careful, even pedantic. And, for good measure, he had sent the first drafts of the manuscript to Gail Rebuck (his wife and a book publisher), Alastair Campbell (his friend and a former journalist) and Tony Blair (a former Prime Minister and, by then, an author) to check the manuscript, line by line. The result was a page-turner. And it was a love letter – to Gail, to Georgia and Grace, to life.

A few days later, Keith Blackmore, the deputy editor, and I visited Philip at his home just off Regent's Park to discuss how we would run it in the paper. Keith is what, in journalism, passes for a renaissance man, a heroically well-read autodidact with hugely catholic tastes, a man of formidable decency, thoughtful generosity, a mischievous wit and as debilitating a weakness for Chelsea FC as Philip had for QPR. It was, perhaps, no surprise that the two of them got on. In fact, from that meeting on, it was Keith who shepherded Philip's work into the paper. He saw that

Philip's manuscript could be treated as something more than a memoir, but as a thriller. Each phase of the story ended with a cliffhanger: a diagnosis, an operation, a remission, a return of the cancer, a reprieve again. And over the coming weeks, the two of them worked on it, relentlessly, to and fro, honing the piece for publication. The success of that partnership was such that Keith was asked, on Philip's posthumous instruction, to edit the full and final account of his time in the 'Death Zone'. The result was the extraordinary book, *When I Die*.

Philip's story ran over four full pages of the paper for five days through the course of a week in mid July. The series – it was renamed 'The Unfinished Life', an echo of Philip's book *The Unfinished Revolution* – was puffed on the front page of the paper, using the bold, block capitals usually associated with a tabloid shocker. It looked different. It was. When he had called me towards the end of 2010 and said he wanted to write something about his cancer, I told him we'd run whatever he wrote. I did not know what he had in mind. What we got was something which, in so many ways, took us into new territory. It was a dispatch in the tradition of William Howard Russell's reportage from the Crimea: it was long, it was in the first person and it was from the frontline of a campaign that no one had reported in such a way before.

In the weeks and months that followed, I kept on stopping round at Philip and Gail's home. The visits would always follow the same routine. We would wander into the kitchen, where I would glance at the grid on the fridge that laid out what medicines Philip had to take and when. I would get a glass of water, he would get a cup of green tea (which would sit, undrunk, in front of him). We would go upstairs and sit on the great green sofas in their living room. Each time, Philip took up the same spot, with his back to the window and Regent's Park, and the same pose, stretching backwards, his long legs perched on the coffee table. He talked as he thought and thought as he talked, all the while looking, not at you, but straight ahead into the middle distance. It is a privilege to be a journalist, to sit with people, ask them questions and listen to their answers. Often, you do not realise it at the time. In Philip's case, you did. You knew that you were exceptionally fortunate to be in the room.

These meetings took a more urgent, intense turn after the summer. On 30 August, I got a note from Philip:

James,

Welcome back. There is some good news and some bad news.

The good news is that I understand that you are serialising my new edition of the Unfinished Revolution. I was very keen for it to go to the Times but did not want to push it too much personally. I wanted the book to stand or fall on its own feet. It was great that Little Brown were able to organise a deal. It also means a bit more money for Mike Griffin if it all comes off!

The bad news is that my cancer has returned. We only heard a week ago and I have been in the Marsden since then. They had a whole treatment plan ready for the recurrence and that is happening. Hope to be out later in the week, but this is definitely the last stage. I will be keeping going for a while yet though with any luck.

Gail has been fantastic and was here most of the weekend. She is a star. I have promised Rachel S an interview if you take the book and I want to do that, health permitting (which it should be).

Please don't worry. It was a hell of a week but we got through it.

Very best,
   Philip

Before publication of his series in *The Times*, Philip had talked quite a bit about how he had tried to understand 'the purpose' of this cancer. Tony Blair, he said, had urged him to do so – to try to understand what the illness was calling him to do. After the first diagnosis and, then, after the cancer's initial return, Philip said he had found its purpose in binding him much more closely to his family. This idea of finding your purpose was the recurrent theme during the conversations we had in the final weeks of Philip's life. He asked it of himself, of me and, come to think of it, he came to ask it of Tony Blair – in that friendship, it felt as if the teacher had become the student in those last weeks. For

Philip had found a purpose that arguably transcended all the political advice he had previously given: it was to enable people to see death as an essential, perhaps the essential, moment in life. I remember him saying to me that death, rather than birth, was the rite of passage that we should celebrate. If birth was a moment pregnant with possibility, death was freighted with experiences and relationships. It was a defining moment in life. True enough, this glass-half-full approach to the end of life struck me as a statement of personality rather than philosophy: if Philip's political outlook was rooted in anything, it was a belief in the self-fulfilling power of optimism. (It was why he was a devotee of Tony Blair. It was, for all their differences on policy, why he had regard for David Cameron.)

Philip described the moment that the doctors told him he was entering what he came to call 'the death zone'. The worst-case scenario, they had said to him, was that he had three months to live. The best case? He had three months to live. Until then, he had felt that in the race against cancer he was like Indiana Jones, running away from a rolling ball but with a glimpse of light at the end of the tunnel. In that moment, he said, it was as if a rock had been rolled over that small gateway in the distance and he was left in hopeless darkness. He talked about how he felt suffocated by it. But, then, he went on to talk about the next three days he spent in a hospital bedroom with Gail, describing what he called 'The Reckoning' of their life together: the first day, they reminisced for hours about all that had happened between; the second, he said, Gail blamed him for all he had done wrong and, for the first time, he took it, he didn't make his previous excuses or equivocations, but owned his shortcomings and apologised; the third day, they sat and discussed the future of Gail's life after he was gone. This was to hear a man talk, deeply, of love. He recounts it all in *When I Die*. And, in fact, all of what he sought to do – in giving purpose to his death, in making sure that, for himself and his family, he had a good one – is expressed in the words of Gail, Georgia and Grace in that book: the indelible moment of which was Gail's remark at the moment he died: 'Philip, I didn't know it would be so beautiful.'

The last time we met, he suggested that, on my next visit, we should go up to Highgate to visit the plot he had chosen for his burial. He had been recently with his sister and then, again, with an old friend. He loved the location, under the cherry tree and towards the end of a row of great Victorian tombstones. He talked excitedly about the beautiful headstone that Matthew Freud had helped commission. Philip loved the art of it, but just wanted it to be bigger. Highgate Cemetery, he felt, was a measure of how Britons saw themselves: the Victorians had grand, ornate headstones that spoke of the sweeping sense of their own ambition; the post-war graves were all low and unassuming; in fact, borderline apologetic. Philip wanted his grave to be in the Victorian mould: he wanted it large and aspiring.

I never got to go with Philip up to Highgate. He died on 6 November 2011. *The Times* published his obituary the following day, as well as a leader, titled 'The Optimist'. It read:

Philip Gould had so much to live for. A wife he loved deeply; daughters he was proud of and whose success he was watching with pride; politics he believed in and causes he knew he could make a difference to. And he was only 61 when he died. He had reached the stage in life and a status that might allow him to relax just a little, and enjoy what he had strived to create.

Yet when he was told that he had just three months to live, this man who had so much to live for still found the upside in dying. He still found something to wonder at, and revel in, and be optimistic about.

He said that being told he had only days left to him, brought an intensity to his life which he could not have experienced in any other way.

Lord Gould of Brookwood was able to see the world that way because he was a remarkable man. He was a romantic, scouring the battlefield for a charger to mount and a tattered standard to raise. But he was also a clear eyed realist, determined to see the world as it is and force others to do so. Realist and romantic, a most unusual combination.

And one that changed British politics and made him a pioneering political figure. In his memoirs The Unfinished Revolution, Gould records that he didn't grow up in places with a great political tradition, or dramatic folklore. He grew up in Woking in Surrey, 'an unexceptional suburban town'. His lifelong political romance was with places like Woking, and his lifelong political contribution came from his understanding of the realities of living in such places.

Philip Gould rose in politics just as the old certainties of the post-war era began to crumble. He was able to see, quite early, the challenge this posed to Labour, and the opportunity it offered. He saw that the rise of the suburban middle class had made traditional democratic socialism redundant. But he saw, too, that this rising class, though not unionised, though working in office blocks and call centres not factories, owning more than one television, and driving family cars, did not think of itself as comfortable or prosperous. The left, he felt, could speak for these people.

And so he began to argue, with the intensity and obsessive drive that, coupled with captivating charm, characterised him, that Labour had to change. He found it a frustrating experience until he found a soul mate in Tony Blair.

Under Gould's influence, as well, of course, as Mr Blair's, politics in Britain changed profoundly. Gould helped develop a Labour which came to terms with market economics, used tougher rhetoric about crime and welfare and was firmly Atlanticist. In Tony Blair's inner circle, Gould was the most convinced that this new approach was right and was critical to his adoption.

Gould's argument that political parties must understand social change and adapt to it eventually became of importance to the right. Through his writing and example, he inspired the modernisers surrounding David Cameron.

In his last year he wrote movingly of his last great campaign. He fought against his cancer with every political weapon he had developed, he organised against it, he tried to understand it, he gathered the finest professionals to fight it.

He never denied what cancer was, its terrible reality, but he never lost the ability to see what it could give to him, as well as what it could take from him. There is a victory in that.

Index

Compiled by Sue Carlton